D0532375

OPEN-AIR EVANGELISM
A PRACTICAL HANDBOOK

Mark Howe
(Editor)

FOREWORD BY IAN BARCLAY

Illustrations by Adrian Barclay

CHRISTIAN LITERATURE CRUSADE
51, The Dean, Alresford, Hants. SO24 9BJ

Open-Air Evangelism: A Practical Handbook

© 1991 Open Air Campaigners (GB)
First UK edition 1991

ISBN 0900284617

Cover design by Rob Wright

The Editor of this work has asserted his moral rights in accordance
with the Copyright Act 1988

All rights reserved. No part of this publication may be reproduced
in any form without the written permission of the publisher.
Christian Literature Crusade, 51, The Dean, Alresford, Hants. SO24 9BJ

Scripture quotations are taken from The Holy Bible, New
International Version. Copyright 1973, 1984 International Bible
Society. Used by permission of Hodder & Stoughton Ltd.

Phototypeset by Intype, London
Printed in England by Clays Ltd, St Ives plc

Table of Contents

Part IV: Reaching children in the open air

Part V: Additional techniques

Part VI: Resources

Foreword

Today I heard about a group of Christians who hold an open-air meeting every Saturday afternoon in the local shopping arcade, but sadly they spend the time entertaining themselves with worship and a loud deliverance ministry with little or no attempt to reach the outsider. Yet I suppose, they are one step ahead of the fellowship that never even tries to mobilise its membership and get them outside the confines of the building they use every Sunday.

Our country is full of sites that can readily be used for a successful open-air ministry. I have always been intrigued by the *Open Air Campaigners* use of the sketchboard, so when Mark Howe's book reached me I didn't have to be persuaded to read it.

We are at the beginning of a *Decade for Evangelism*. I would therefore have thought that *Open-Air Evangelism* is essential reading for every P.C.C. and church committee member. Certainly no minister or pastor can afford to be without it as a resource and "how to" book. In local evangelism we are still majoring on what Gavin Reid used to call "in-drag" instead of "outreach". Yet here is a book which in the most practical way can equip the ordinary church member so that he or she can get out into the marketplace of the local community with the message of Jesus Christ.

Mark Howe argues the case for open-air ministry. There is an emphasis on sketchboard ministry, which I personally feel is a winner in terms of attention holding and presenting the Gospel in a contemporary way. But other methods are touched on too, such as music, drama, conjuring, escapology and ventriloquism. Mark Howe also deals with all the logistical problems, from choosing a site and the role of team members, to the invitation and follow up.

Open-Air Evangelism: A Practical Handbook is a straightforward, unfussy, clearly presented, well illustrated, easy to follow resource book, designed to equip the ordinary church member. I will certainly make sure that my local minister and mission committee has a copy. Do the same for your church.

Ian Barclay
Minister At Large For The Evangelical Alliance

Acknowledgements

Much of the material presented here has been created and collated, researched and refined, taught and even translated by hundreds of evangelists over at least the last sixty years. In addition, they and many others have used the theories and the good ideas in the course of their ministry, transforming them into tested methods which God has used to enlarge his kingdom. With such a rich background, assembling the information into a book was the easy part!

I would like to thank those who has prepared material for this handbook, including Dawn Clancy, Mark Detzler, David Fanstone, Mike Getley, Peter Hodge, Susan Howe, Pauline Nix and Simon Ponsonby. In addition to references in the reading list I have made use of various seminar notes, and I have found those of Julian Richards to be particularly useful. Thanks to my wife Susan for typing most of the manuscript, and to the many people inside and outside OAC who have read previous versions, chased references and provided useful suggestions.

On a more personal level I am very grateful to the various members of Open Air Campaigners who have been willing to share their godly wisdom with me during my training, and especially to Graham Simms, who led the first OAC training course I attended. Special thanks are also due to Korky Davey, who risked having me on his team, and to all those at OAC West Country. I have appreciated the opportunity to learn with and from colleagues who have also become good friends, particularly Martin Blewett, David Buick, Mark Detzler and Stephen Poulard. My wife Susan has contributed in many ways, but most of all by just being there, while my long-suffering family has never stopped loving and caring. Susan and I could never have joined OAC were it not for the support of several churches and many individuals who have prayed, given and encouraged in so many practical ways.

Most importantly, I acknowledge that ultimately all the thanks must go to God. I thank him for a new life, for the Gospel I seek to communicate and for the Holy Spirit, the partner of all evangelists, without whose work the best techniques and most eloquent words are worse than useless.

Introduction

The material in this handbook has been divided into six major parts:

Part I (Historical and biblical context) provides the background to the rest of the handbook.

Part II (Using a sketchboard) describes the techniques and equipment involved in using a sketchboard.

Part III (Reaching adults in the open air) builds on part II and covers various aspects of open-air evangelism for adults.

Part IV (Reaching children in the open air) also assumes familiarity with the material in part II, and covers various aspects of open-air evangelism for children.

Part V (Additional techniques) introduces five other forms of communication which are sometimes used as part of an open-air programme.

Part VI (Resources) contains messages, drawings, programmes and other ideas for use in the open air.

The most important word in the title of this

handbook is "practical". It is assumed that the reader will wish to use the information presented here to proclaim the Gospel. Those looking for an exhaustive history of open-air evangelism will have to continue their search, as will those requiring a review of all possible Christian activities in the open air. The reading list may help, although it must be admitted that little material has been published on these subjects. The treatment of additional techniques in part V is also necessarily brief, and those wishing to use such techniques will need to consult other sources.

Finally, a few comments about the conventions followed in this handbook. Male pronouns have been used throughout to refer to people in general: this has been done simply to avoid clumsy constructions such as (s)he or him/her, and is not intended to make any theological or sociological point. The messages in the resources section are written as they might be preached, and so some of the normal rules of written grammar have been ignored.

About Open Air
Campaigners in Europe

Open Air Campaigners (OAC) is a missionary
society which specialises in taking the Good News
of Jesus Christ to people where they are. From
its beginnings OAC has been interdenominational,
relying upon the support of churches and individuals.

The ministry of OAC began in Australia in 1892,
the current name being adopted in 1922. Today we

also work in over a dozen countries including New Zealand, USA, Canada and virtually every country in Western Europe. The International Board of Reference includes many of those at the forefront of world evangelism today.

An increasing number of Europeans live in large towns and cities. Because of their increasingly complex lifestyles and the subsequent problems in reaching them, much of OAC's work takes place in the open air. OAC evangelists present the Gospel in shopping centres, parks, high streets, markets . . . in short almost anywhere that people gather.

There is only one Gospel, but there are many ways of presenting it! OAC uses a variety of methods to confront people with the Good News of Jesus Christ. Many of those reached have had little or no contact with the Church.

In the 1950s an OAC evangelist called Jim Duffecy visited the Royal Sydney Show, where he saw an artist using a large sketchboard to advertise famous products. The artist used a special style of writing called "ladder lettering", and Jim realised that a similar technique could be used to present the Gospel.

Today the sketchboard is almost the "trademark" of Open Air Campaigners. The combination of sound scriptural preaching and powerful visual aids has been used by God all over the world. Adults and children alike are being converted, discipled and linked with local churches.

Of course OAC recognises that no one method of communication is ideal for all situations, and so our evangelists will often be found using street drama, music or ventriloquism in the course of their work. We frequently work alongside other churches and societies, providing specialist training and leadership in frontline evangelism.

As well as open-air work, OAC evangelists across Europe work in a wide variety of situations ranging from prisons to church pulpits, from schools to retirement homes and from children's holiday clubs to radio and television studios. OAC has a "give-away" ministry, and our evangelists spend much of their time training local churches, missionary societies and individuals in effective evangelism. Training seminars are held at many Bible Colleges.

For further information about the work of OAC please contact:

David Fanstone, 102 Dukes Avenue, Muswell Hill, London N10 2QA

Illustrations

Illustrations

Part I:
Historical and biblical context

1: What is evangelism?

"To evangelise is to spread the Good News that Jesus Christ died for our sins and was raised from the dead according to the Scriptures, and that as reigning Lord he now offers the forgiveness of sins and the liberating gift of the Spirit to all who repent and believe. . ."[1]

"To evangelise is to present Christ Jesus to sinful men in order that, through the power of the Holy Spirit, they may come to put their trust in God through him, to accept him as their Saviour and to serve him as their king in the fellowship of his church."[2]

The role of the evangelist in the New Testament is often similar to that of the Old Testament prophet. God calls his servants to present his message to the nations:

"Assemble the people – men, women and children, and the aliens living in your towns – so that they can listen and learn to fear the Lord your

---

1. Section 4 of the Lausanne Covenant, quoted in The Fisherman's Basket (see reading list).
2. J.I. Packer, Evangelism and the Sovereignty of God, pp37,38,40, IVP, quoted in D. Watson, I believe in evangelism, Hodder & Stoughton, 1986.

God and follow carefully all the words of this law."
Deut 31:12.

Jesus continued the prophetic tradition by pro-
claiming the Gospel publicly (Matt 4:23). In the
Great Commission he commanded his disciples to
do the same (Matt 28:18–19) and promised to be
with them in this context (Matt 28:20). It was as
the disciples obeyed that they had the privilege of
working in partnership with God (Mark 16:20).
Although modern societies are often quite different
from biblical Israel the same principles hold true
today.

The idea of partnership with God in evangelism
must be grasped if we are to avoid unnecessary
worry and disappointment. Mark 16:20 spells out
the responsibilities of the disciples and of the Holy
Spirit. The disciples went out and preached everywhere. In other words they obeyed the Great
Commission, leaving the security of their friends
and family in order to announce the Good News.
The briefest study of the book of Acts shows that
their success in terms of conversions or disciples
was decidedly variable. In some places thousands
repented (eg Acts 2:41). In other places the reponse
was less spectacular (eg Acts 17:34), while on
occasions their preaching was apparently misun-
derstood and they barely escaped with their lives
(eg Acts 14:19). One lesson to be drawn from this
is that a powerful testimony, a clever technique or
a sacrificial prayer life will not always guarantee a
large positive response to the Gospel. God calls us
to obey him, not to try to force his hand.

The second half of Mark 16:20 explains the part
that the Holy Spirit plays in evangelism. ". . . the

Lord worked with them and confirmed his word by the signs that accompanied it". It is the Holy Spirit who can convict people of their sinfulness (John 16:8). The Holy Spirit is involved in choosing those who will respond to God (1 Pet 1:2). And it was in the power of the Holy Spirit that the disciples were able to perform the miraculous signs which were always an accompaniment and complement to, rather than a substitute for their preaching (Acts 6:4).

Proclamation and personal contact are two key ingredients of effective evangelism. For example, when Peter preached his first recorded Gospel message he spoke to a large crowd (Acts 2:14). However the communication was not one-way: people asked questions (Acts 2:37), and Peter warned them and pleaded with them (Acts 2:40). Jesus was willing to spend time with individuals as well as with the masses (eg John 3 and 4).

Unfortunately, there is often a disturbing contrast between the excitement of evangelism in the early Church and our own experience. There are a number of reasons why evangelistic efforts fail. Firstly, the Gospel must not be distorted. For example some evangelists succumb to the temptation of playing down the sinfulness of man and the need for repentance in the hope of making the Gospel more acceptable. The "converts" are then in for a shock when they start to attend church or read the Bible and discover that they have responded to only half the message. Similarly the stereotype of an open-air preacher for too many people is a man in a black suit screaming a sermon of hellfire and damnation at startled passers-by.

5

We need to proclaim a balanced Gospel to produce balanced disciples.

Secondly, it is important to use the right methods. There can be no room for compromise of our message, but often we convince ourselves that the same applies to the way in which we convey that message. Society is changing at a faster rate than ever before, and we need to be looking constantly for the best ways to communicate to modern men and women. It is possible to be too concerned with methods, and God in his grace often uses anachronistic or amateurish attempts at evangelism, but nonetheless we should not become complacent.

A third problem is quite simply motivation. It is more comfortable for us to stay in our churches or pay a "professional" to do our evangelism for us than to become involved ourselves. Obedience to Christ's call has always been costly, and the world will be reached as quickly or as slowly as you and I are willing to obey and pay the price.

When regular evangelism takes place, it can be expected that contacts will be made. Some of these contacts will be converted and become involved in the local church. The profile of the church in its community will be raised and church members will be encouraged. However, the primary motivation must always be a desire to serve God, and not to build an earthly empire.

2: Why Evangelism?

Because Jesus commands it

From the beginning of his own ministry Jesus spent much of his time preaching the Good News (Matt 4:17,23). He told his disciples to pray that God would send workers into the harvest fields (Matt 9:37–38) and then sent them out to do exactly the same things that he himself had been doing (Matt 10). His last command was to go and make disciples from all nations (Matt 28:18–20).

Because that's how the early Church grew

When the Holy Spirit came at Pentecost, Peter was quick to use the interest generated as a chance to proclaim the Gospel (Acts 2:14). 3000 people responded to this one sermon (Acts 2:41). After a healing Peter preached again, and by this time the Church had grown to about 5000 men plus their families (Acts 4:4). They were willing to risk everything to tell others about Jesus (Acts 4:18–19), and threats only increased their desire to speak out (Acts 4:29). The believers were soon scattered all over Judea and Samaria (Acts 8:1), but they took this as an opportunity to preach to a wider audience (Acts 8:4). The Church sent out people to reach all parts of the Roman Empire (eg Acts 13:1–5). Within 100 years of the resurrection of Jesus there were hundreds of local fellowships covering much of the Empire.

Because the Church today needs it

The Church in Europe today is in a far weaker position than in previous times. One Christian leader has placed the proportion of "proficient" Christians in Britain today at around 2%.[3] Christians no longer have the same influence on society which they once had. Evangelism has always been one important reason for the existence of the Church, and where churches fail to reach out to their neighbours, other areas of church life often suffer. In fact evangelism will enhance all aspects of the Church (Eph 4:11–13).

Because the world today needs it

Jesus called his disciples to be salt in their society (Matt 5:13). One of the main uses of salt in the ancient world was to prevent food from rotting. Where Christians have failed to take an interest in those outside the Church, both through teaching how Christ can change individuals and through encouraging Christian standards of behaviour, society starts to decay. Other religions such as Islam and philosophies such as the New Age movement are attracting many followers in Europe

3. David Pawson, "Cutting Edge", *Leadership Today*, May 1987.

because there is a commitment to "sharing the faith" in these groups which is often absent in mainstream Christianity.

Because people are dying without Christ

Jesus tells us that he is the only way for us to know God (John 14:6). Yet millions of people have never had the chance to respond to the Gospel, and so can never know God personally. Those who do not know Jesus as Saviour are in danger of going to hell (Rev 20:15). God expects us to warn everyone about this danger, and holds us responsible if we do not do so (Ezek 33:7–9, 30–33).

3: What is the Gospel?

It is one thing to know what the Gospel is, but quite another to be able to explain it in a concise and meaningful way to someone who has never heard it before. There are dozens of systems for presenting the Gospel. Many of them can be useful, but none of them is perfect, not least because the best style of presentation will depend on the person presenting it and the person hearing it.

By way of illustration two presentations of the Gospel are given below. They are both adapted from leaflets produced by the same author, but the first is intended for use with adults while the second is aimed at children. It might be useful to compare the way different aspects of the Gospel message are dealt with for these two audiences.

Return to God (for adults) by Peter Hodge[4]

Is it possible for me to have a real, lasting and meaningful relationship with God?

...Yes. When God created man he made him perfect. His desire was that we should be his friends and govern the earth, caring for it. God did

4. Return to God (for adults), OAC GB.

not make us robots: he gave us "free will" so that we could choose between right and wrong, good and bad. God wants us to love him and most of all to know him personally: however he does not force us to love him: he wants us to choose. So man has a choice.

Man did choose but he made the wrong choice. "There is a way that seems right to a man but in the end it leads to death." (Prov 14:12) Instead of doing what God wanted he decided to go his own way, independently of God. The Bible calls this sin.

So mankind became separated from God through sin, and became selfish, unkind, empty and purposeless. We are still separated from God, because even today we choose to disobey and go our own way.

"For out of the heart come evil thoughts. . ." (Matt 15:19)

"For all have sinned and come short of the glory (perfection) of God." (Rom 3:23).

"Your iniquities (waywardness) have separated you from God; your sins have hidden his face from you so that he will not hear." (Isa 59:2).

We try to solve this problem ourselves. Are you trying any of these ways: good works; morality; philosophy; religion? There is only one remedy for the problem. Sin has to be dealt with. "God has shown how much he loves us, it was while we were yet sinners that Christ died for us." (Rom 5:8)

Jesus Christ is God's only acceptable answer to the problem of man's sin. "Salvation is found in no-one else, for there is no other name under

11

heaven given to men by which we must be saved."
(Acts 4:12)

When Jesus took the punishment for our sins on
the cross and died in our place, it was as if he took
the hand of God and our hand and reconciled us
both in his death. In so doing he bridged the gap
of separation and dealt with man's problem of sin
once and for all. "God was reconciling the world
to himself in Christ . . . God made him who had
no sin to be sin for us. . ." (2 Cor 5:19,21) "He
himself bore our sins in his body on the tree." (1
Pet 2:24)

Jesus was born to die: we were born to live.
Jesus not only died for our sins but rose again to
prove without any doubt that he was victorious
over sin and death. "He was delivered over to
death for our sins and was raised to life for our
justification." (Rom 4:25) This was to guarantee
that his sacrificial death was accepted by God.

The big question now is: can God's only answer
become effective for me? The answer is Yes! You
must be willing to turn from sin (repent), to put
your personal trust in Jesus Christ and make him
Lord of your life. Do not think you can enter into
all that God has planned for you in any other way:
nothing and no-one else can bridge that gap. Jesus
said, "I am the Way and the Truth and the Life,
no-one comes to the Father except through me."
(John 14:6)

Where do you stand? Is your life full of sin,
separation, frustration, guilt, lack of purpose? Are
you heading for hell? Would you like to experience
the forgiveness, eternal and abundant life, pardon

and purpose that God offers? Would you like to be sure of going to heaven?

Is there any reason why you should not take this important step of choosing God's way right now and of putting your trust in his Son? God gives these promises and warnings:

"He who has the Son has life, he who does not have the Son does not have life." (1 John 5:12)

"If you confess with your mouth, 'Jesus is Lord' and believe in your heart that God raised him from the dead you will be saved." (Romans 10:9)

Before Jesus ascended into heaven he promised to send the Holy Spirit who would live in Christians and give them power and the ability to live as they should. (Acts 1:8)

To enter into God's way it's as simple as ABC.

A: Admit that you are wrong (sinner) and be willing to turn from your sins (repent).

B: Believe God's only provision is in Jesus – his death and resurrection.

C: Commit your life to him, put your faith and trust in Jesus.

If you mean business then God is now only a prayer away. Why not take that step right now? You might find this prayer helpful:

Dear God,

I admit I am a sinner and need your forgiveness; I believe that Jesus Christ died in my place paying the penalty for my sins; I am willing right now to turn from my sin and accept Jesus Christ as my personal Saviour and Lord. I commit myself to you and ask you to send the Holy Spirit into my life, to fill me and take control, and to help me become the kind of person you want me to be. Thank you Father for loving me. In Jesus' name. Amen

This is what has happened. Because you have repented and put your faith and trust in Jesus your sins are forgiven. You have become a member of God's family. You have been filled with the Holy Spirit to enable you to live a victorious life in his power. God has a lot more planned for you as a member of his family so be open and available to him.

Having sincerely chosen to follow the Lord Jesus Christ, you have begun a new life in his family. God promises his children a lot of things in the Bible. Here are just a few:

"All those who trust him – God's Son – to save them have eternal life. (John 3:36)

"Anyone who calls upon the name of the Lord will be saved." (Rom 10:13)

"God has said 'Never will I leave you, never will I forsake you' " (Heb 13:5)

"I give to them eternal life and they shall never perish, no-one can snatch them out of my hand." (John 10:28)

"To all who received him, to those who believed in his name, he gave the right to become children of God." (John 1:12)

Further Important Steps for New Christians

The Bible tells you:
– CONFESS your mistakes and wrongdoings in prayer (1 John 1:9).

- Be FILLED with the Holy Spirit (Ephesians 5:18).
- READ and STUDY the BIBLE (ask the Holy Spirit to help you) and OBEY what he tells you to do (2 Timothy 2:15).
- Be BAPTISED as soon as possible (Acts 10:48).
- MEET with other Christians for worship and encouragement (Hebrews 10:25).
- Speak to God in PRAYER (Philippians 4:6).
- TELL others the Good News: you cannot have a monopoly on the Gospel (1 Peter 3:15)!

Return to God (for children) by Peter Hodge[5]

God loves you and thinks you are very special. He's got a lot of great things planned for you and he wants you to be his child, to live with him now and for ever (he calls this eternal life). "For I know the plans I have for you, says the Lord. They are plans for good and not for evil, to give you a future and a hope." (Jer 29:11)

Most boys and girls are not enjoying God's special plan for their life, because of sin. Sin is wanting to go your own way and not God's, and each of us have done that. "We all, like sheep, have gone astray, each of us has turned to his own way. . . ." (Isa 53:6)

We do things wrong because of wrong things in our hearts (lives).

"Out of the heart of man come bad thoughts." (Mark 7:21) "Your sins have separated you from God." (Isa 59:2)

5. Return to God (for children), OAC GB.

15

To be able to enjoy all that God has got planned for us we must deal first of all with the problem. We can't!... But God has!

Jesus Christ is God's son. He has never sinned. He came from heaven to this earth, and when he died on the cross, he was allowing God to punish him for all our sins. The Bible says, "Christ died for our sins." (1 Cor 15:3)

Jesus was buried. On the third day he came back to life. Jesus is alive today. Before he went back to heaven he promised to send the Holy Spirit, who will live in all those who trust in Jesus giving them power and ability to live as he wants them to. (Acts 1:8)

Would you like to have all your bad thoughts, words and deeds forgiven? Would you like to start enjoying the fantastic new life that God has planned for you? Would you like to become a member of God's family for ever? You would? Well that's great!

To enter into God's way, it's as simple as ABC:

A: Admit that you are wrong – tell God you are sorry for your sins and that you want to go his way.

B: Believe that Jesus died on the cross for your sin and rose again.

C: Commit your life to him. Put your faith and trust in Jesus.

The Bible says all who trust him (God's Son) to save them have Eternal Life (John 3:36)

If you would like to take these important steps here is a prayer you can use:

What is the Gospel?

Dear God,

I am sorry for all my sins and I want to go your way. Thank you that you died on the cross and were punished in my place so that I could be forgiven. I am willing right now to turn from all I know to be wrong and put my trust in you, Jesus Christ, as my Saviour and Lord. Please make my life clean and send the Holy Spirit to fill me and take control. Help me to become the kind of person you want me to be. In Jesus' name, Amen.

Congratulations! This is what has happened. Because you have repented of your sins (that means being sorry enough not to do it again) and put your faith and trust in Jesus, your sins are forgiven. You have become a member of God's family. You have been filled with the Holy Spirit to enable you to live a victorious life in his power. God has a lot more planned for you as a member of his family so be open and available to him.

Here are some of God's promises for you:

"I will never leave you. . ." (Heb 13:5)
"I give them eternal life, and they shall never perish; no-one can snatch them out of my hand." (John 10:28)
"To all who received him, to those who believed in his name, he gave the right to become children of God." (John 1:12)

Further important tips for keeping to the right pathway:

1. Talk to God every day (that's called praying), own up to your sin (1 John 1:9); thank Jesus that he died for that sin too! Ask the Holy Spirit for his help and to fill you daily.
2. Read the Bible every day and ask the Holy Spirit (who lives in you now) to help you. If he tells you to do something then obey.
3. Tell others the Good News about Jesus.
4. Go to a good Church or Sunday School as often as possible and meet with others who love the Lord Jesus.

4: Visual aids in the Bible and history

Are visual aids biblical?

This should be a serious question for any evangelical Christian. The fact that visual aids can be effective does not necessarily justify their use in a Christian context, as the end can never justify the means. We have already seen that God deigns to use fallible men and women to accomplish his perfect purpose, and so the success of any evangelistic endeavour tells us more about the grace of God than about the inherent "soundness" of human strategies.

It must be conceded from the outset that there is no recorded instance of Jesus or the apostles using a sketchboard in the course of their ministry! However arguments from silence are always rather weak, and it is more productive to consider the principles of communication that are shown in the Old and New Testaments.

It is clear from the first five books of the New Testament that the ministry of Jesus and the early Church was by no means limited to oral communication. Alongside the teaching and preaching are

19

nature miracles (eg Matt 8:26, Acts 12:5–7), the exercise of power over demons (eg Matt 17:18, Acts 16:18) and healings (eg Matt 4:23, Acts 3:7). Moreover, the biblical account presents all these aspects of the Church's ministry as an integrated whole, rather than as a list of alternatives. New Testament preachers were not slow to use events around them as a basis for their preaching. Jesus' parables were drawn from everyday life, and a freak accident was used to teach on repentance (Luke 13:1–3). It is also difficult to see the cursing of the fig tree as anything but an impressive visual demonstration (Matt 21:18–22). Jesus even describes his resurrection as a sign (Luke 11:29). Peter made the most of the Pentecost outpouring and the healing at the Beautiful Gate to preach (Acts 2:14–16, 3:11–13).

While it should be clear from the above that early Church communication was a multi-media phenomenon, there is a danger of ignoring other reasons for the actions of God and man. Although it is clear that the miracles and healings of Jesus did convey spiritual truth and attracted crowds (eg Matt 4:24–25), the primary motivation was his compassion for the needy and their loved ones (Matt 14:14, 20:34, Mark 1:41, Mark 8:2). It is also worth noting that sometimes the miracles were not well received (eg Acts 16:16–19).

The use of visual aids is even clearer in the Old Testament. Moses was not prepared to speak to Pharaoh's court without three different signs to support his message (Exod 4:1–9). Hosea was commanded to marry an adulterous woman, and then to buy her back from slavery in order to demonstrate the forgiveness of God (Hos 1:2, 3:1–3). Isaiah was told to remove all his clothes and walk around naked and barefoot for three years, before the Lord explained the point of the illustration (Isa 20:1–4)! Jeremiah used a yoke to illustrate the approaching servitude of Judah, while Ezekiel was commanded to use a variety of dramatic means to demonstrate God's word for Jerusalem (Ezek 3–12). One commentary on the book of Ezekiel notes that, "The value of visual aids has been more fully appreciated in recent years as a means of reinforcing the message of the spoken word. God was well aware of the value centuries ago and made full use of it in teaching his people his plans and purposes and in conveying his warnings to them."[6]

It is important to note that most of the illustrations mentioned above had no value apart from educational. In the light of the forms of communication used by the Prophets which sometimes contravened social and even religious norms (eg Isa 20:1–4, Ezek 4:9–15), most of the ideas in use today seem somewhat tame!

Are visual aids necessary?

It is sometimes argued that even if visual aids can be justified from Scripture, they are an unnecessary distraction from the important work of preaching the Word. After all, the great open-air preachers of past centuries used to captivate massive crowds solely by the eloquence of their anointed speech. And isn't there a danger that the listener will go

6. Dr Fredk., A. Tatford, Dead bones live: an exposition of Ezekiel's prophecy, Prophetic Witness Publishing House, 1977.

away thinking more of the visual aid than of the message?

In the first place, it must be noted that by no means all Christian communication since the apostles has relied solely on the spoken word. The brass bands of the Salvation Army must have once caused the same misgivings that some feel today towards the use of contemporary music by the church. Their musical style was intended to be something which the irreligious working-class would relate to. Even the caricature of a Victorian missionary includes a blackboard and chalks alongside the pith helmet.

Secondly, the society to which we proclaim the Gospel has changed. In particular, the average Western adult is used to information being presented in short, pre-digested helpings, always in full colour and preferably in animation. The church service must be one of the last remaining contexts in which modern man encounters a thirty-minute block of solid oratory. There is an irony in the fact that the place where visual aids are usually most easily accepted within a church is in the Sunday school, and yet schoolchildren are probably more accustomed to listening to monologues, taking notes and learning from dusty books than their parents, to whom no alternative is presented!

Thirdly, there is evidence to show that certain types of information can be more easily absorbed when presented visually. Anyone who has ever tried to describe a diagram of even a modestly complex item by telephone will confirm this. Road signs, maps and diagrams of electronic circuits are all examples of non-linguistic forms of communication which have found widespread acceptance. On a more serious note, great tragedies often come to be synonymous with a press photo which is then used to summarise all the facts, statistics and emotions surrounding the event. A picture is often worth at least a thousand words.

Fourthly, it is possible to deduce a lot from looking at the tactics of advertisers. Of course it is dangerous to push the analogy between evangelism and advertising to extremes, but nonetheless it is likely that companies continue to pour huge sums of money into television, posters and colour hand-bills because such techniques bring tangible results. Certainly they have no interest in beguiling people with the medium if the message is not being received.

In summary, God has always used a variety of means to reach out to mankind. Throughout biblical and modern history these means have often been visual. The rest of this handbook shows how visual aids can be used in the open air to present the Good News in a powerful way.

5: The case for open-air evangelism

It has been used with great success throughout history

The patriarchs and prophets often taught and preached to the people in the open air (eg Deut 1). John the Baptist spent much of his ministry preaching in the wilderness (John 1:3), and Jesus preached his most famous sermon on a hillside (Matt 5:1). The early Church grew though many forms of evangelism, including open-air preaching (Acts 3:11, Acts 17:17). When the Church was scattered (Acts 8:1) the followers of Jesus preached the Gospel wherever they went (Acts 8:4). Even when Paul was under arrest (Acts 21:40) he took the opportunity to preach outside the barracks.

In times of great revival God has used open-air preachers such as John Wesley and George White-field to reach thousands of people outside the Church. C.H. Spurgeon used to tell his students, "No sort of defence is needed for preaching out of doors, but it would need very potent arguments to prove that a man had done his duty who has never preached beyond the walls of his meeting house.

A defence is required rather for services within buildings than for worship outside of them."[7] Today God still uses open-air evangelism all over the world.

It is ideal for use in cities

An increasingly large percentage of the world's population lives in cities and conurbations. Many of those who live in suburbs work and shop in city centres. Open-air evangelism can be used to reach people in parks, shopping precincts, high streets or almost anywhere else that people gather.

7. C.H. Spurgeon, Lectures to my students on the art of preaching XVIII, p254, Marshall, Morgan & Scott, 1986.

The case for open-air evangelism

It can reach large numbers of people

In many parts of the world it is not unusual to collect crowds of several hundred to hear the Gospel. Most of those listening will have had little contact with the Church, compared with crusades, in which the audience is typically 90% Christian. A series of open-air meetings, even of quite a modest size, can reach thousands of people over the course of a year. ˜

It facilitates personal contact

Effective evangelism should always result in a Christian talking to a non-Christian, and in open-air meetings this is relatively easy to arrange. Christians in the crowd can simply turn to the person next to them at the end of a meeting and share Christ with them. Those who are not interested will normally have left by the end of the meeting, and so the counsellors can be confident of having useful conversations.

It is cheap and simple

Open-air evangelism does not require a hall, publicity or security. It can be organised quickly, and can be conducted by members of a local church. The use of the streets is free, and in England it is expressly allowed by law. The equipment is cheap to buy or easy to make.

It is good for the Church

Most people rarely go inside a church, and so open-air evangelism enables them to see Christians who have a living relationship with God and who want to share it. Church members can be involved in open-air evangelism in various ways, and so find and develop their gifts. In particular, the open air is a great place to learn to preach, as the "audience" can walk away!

Part II:
Using a sketchboard

6: Principles of communication

Effective Christian communication involves taking a person from where he is to where you want him to be by the most direct route possible. This process can be broken down into five parts:

Attention. If people are unaware of your existence they are unlikely to respond to your message! Visual aids such as the sketchboard help to catch attention, but remember that you are the best visual aid of all.

Interest. All the sketchboard techniques are designed to create curiosity, but there is no substitute for talking about interesting issues. Jesus took examples from everyday life and used them to explain great spiritual truths. By talking about something which concerns your audience you earn their respect, making it more likely that they will take your message seriously. Choose subjects which have a wide appeal, and about which you know something.

Spiritual concern. The most skilful part of open-air preaching is introducing the Gospel. The temptation is to produce a fascinating presentation with negligible spiritual content, and then suddenly to preach a sermon at the end. This tends to result in the Gospel being pushed further and further to the end of the message and in the audience feeling deceived. Ideally the spiritual content will be introduced gradually. The material in the resources sections illustrates this principle.

Application. The preacher must show the relevance of spiritual truths to the lives of his hearers. Many people are happy to agree with much of the Christian message, but will not accept that it should change their lives. Start with a testimony, to show how God has changed your life. Then talk about people in general, and finally explain the need for a personal response. Be specific, as general statements are hard to apply.

Response. Spell out what you expect people to do. It is important to emphasise that becoming a Christian is primarily about following Christ, not about joining an organisation. See chapter 15 for details of the invitation.

The whole presentation should be between eight and fifteen minutes long. It is possible to cover the essentials of the Gospel in this time, but it requires practice and discipline. Most people talk around subjects, repeating themselves and including a lot of irrelevant detail. A good message will move smoothly from one point to another, presenting the arguments logically and clearly, and delivering devastating content in an attractive way. Chapter 14 explains how to prepare and present a message.

7: Equipment and painting techniques

Sketchbord evangelism does not require expensive equipment, and the evangelist does not need to be an accomplished artist. Nonetheless, a small amount of attention paid to the right choice of equipment and basic technique can make a large difference to the finished result.

Equipment

Sketchboard. The standard sketchboard used in the U.K. is 115cm×76cm (45″×30″). The precise dimensions are not crucial, but the height will be governed by the size of paper which is to be used, while the length is a compromise between maximum painting area, portability and stability. The board typically consists of a 50mm×25mm (2″×1″) wooden frame covered with thin plywood or hardboard. Three blocks of wood are used to mount the aluminium legs. Bulldog clips are used to attach the paper to the board. Several designs of folding board exist, but these may be heavier and less sturdy than a one-piece design. Sketchboards

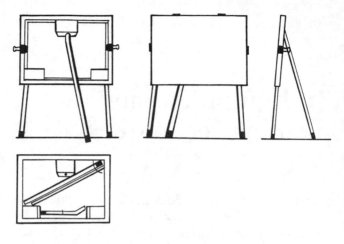

can be bought from several sources, or made by any competent carpenter.

Paper. Newsprint (ie paper used to print newspapers) is ideal. It is cheap (or even free), and is absorbent enough to prevent water-colours from running. It can be obtained from local newspaper print shops.

Attaching the paper to the board, like most things, is simple when you know how! Lay the roll of paper down on a clean smooth surface and slowly pull a length of paper from the roll. Fold the paper over onto itself every 120cm (48″) ie the length of the board plus 3 times the depth. Repeat this as many times as necessary until the required number of sheets have been prepared. Lay the sketchboard on top of the paper (this is easier with two people) so that the bottom of the board is level

34

with one edge of the paper and there is an equal gap either side of the board. Cut diagonally across the top two corners of the board with a sharp pair of scissors. Leaving the board on the paper, slit the folds in one end of the paper with a knife. If the paper used is more than 7.5cm (3″) wider than the height of the board, trim off the excess paper. Fold each cut edge back to the board and fix with bull-dog clips. Then slit the folds at the other side of the board, folding and clipping as before. The diagram below should make this clearer. If the paper is attached carefully the board will look neat, and the paper will be less prone to rip in high winds.

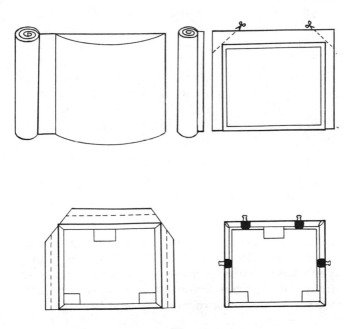

Paintpots. These must be strong and air-tight. Plastic food containers are ideal but baby-food jars can be used if handled carefully. It is not necessary to carry large quantities of paint, but pots should be large enough to stand up with a paintbrush in them.

Paints. These should be water-soluble. Good powder paint or liquid paint of the type used in schools is ideal. Cheap paint is generally not worth buying. Acrylic paints are very bright, but are harder to mix, and can harden if left on the paintbrush. It is best to use basic colours such as yellow, green, red, blue and black. To mix paints, put a small mount of powder or liquid in the bottom of the pot and slowly add water, stirring with a stick or old spoon. Do not use a paintbrush as stirring will damage the bristles. The paints should be tested on a sheet of paper. If the colour is thin, add more paint. If the paint becomes wispy when drawing a long line, add more water. Ensure that when a paintbrush is put in the pot the paint does not rise above the bristles. Paint on the handle will tend to run down onto your hand and arm, to the detriment of the message and the amusement of the crowd!

Brushes. One brush is needed for each colour. Brushes should be oval or chisel-pointed and suitable for use with water colour paints.

Box. This should be big enough to carry paintpots, water and brushes, as well as a cloth for wiping your hands. Fishing-tackle boxes or tool boxes are often suitable. Some way of keeping wet brushes separate during transport must be devised.

Literature. There are two main requirements of literature for open-air meetings. Firstly, it should explain the Gospel in such a way that a person reading it on his own could make an informed commitment to Christ. Secondly, it should contain diagrams or pictures which can be used for counselling, rather than having to read the tract to the contact verbatim. OAC produces a series of tracts for this purpose, but those produced by Agape Europe or Navigators (for example) are also suitable. Literature should always contain some contact address or telephone number.

Painting techniques

Do not pick up the paintpot: leave it in the box. Often old paint will accumulate in the bottom of the box, and this will drip from the pot if it is removed. Dropping a pot of paint during an open-air meeting can be very distracting, and rather costly if you or the crowd are wearing expensive clothes.

Keep your finger away from the bristles: otherwise the paint will soon spread over your hands and clothes.

Stir the paints regularly, as some types of paint are prone to separate out.

Remove excess paint and shape the bristles by wiping the brush on the side of the pot as you pick it up.

Lines should be drawn with the thin edge of the brush. The thickness of the line can be controlled by varying the pressure.

The brush should always be "dragged" rather than pushed.

It is easier to draw straight lines whilst standing about 60cm (2 feet) from the board, rather than with your nose touching the paper.

For backgrounds and special effects, dry brush stroke can be effective. Wipe most of the paint from the brush and gently draw lines to produce a wispy effect.

Ensure that one colour is dry before painting over it with another colour. As a rule light colours should be used before dark colours: black paint will cover mistakes made with yellow paint, but not vice versa.

8: Words and pictures

There is no limit to the variety of pictures which can be painted on the sketchboard. However, some techniques have been found to be particularly useful, and these are described here. The resources in part 6 of this handbook should give further inspiration!

Borders

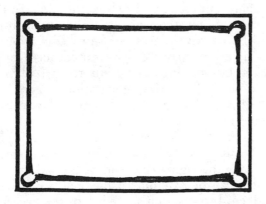

The most common border consists of a yellow frame, round the edge of the board, with a black line drawn inside. Yellow and black provide a striking contrast although other combinations can be tried. A border makes any painting look "finished", and directs attention to the centre of the board.

Lettering

The most popular form of lettering used on the sketchboard is ladder lettering. It is fast to paint, neat, easy to read, and always creates curiosity in those who see it. The "ladder" is painted up before the start of the message, and the letters can then be completed with a few strokes of the paintbrush.

Ladder lettering is most effective when it is simple, and each letter can be painted with no more than four strokes. The boxes for M's and W's should be wider than normal, and those for I's should be narrower. A space should be about the width of a letter, but can be varied according to space limitations. It can be useful to partially-complete some letters during preparation to avoid confusion during the message. Beginners may prefer to pencil in the letters beforehand.

When painting the boxes, which should be about 10cm × 6cm (4″ × 2.5″ or about the size of a cassette box), leave the right-hand end of the ladder open, so that it can be extended if the length required is misjudged. If too much space is left, the excess can be filled in, or turned into exclamation marks or dots.

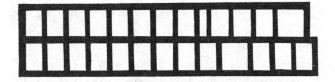

Ladder lettering should be painted in a dark colour such as black, red or blue. Green may also be suitable, depending on the shade of paint chosen. Important words can be emphasised by using a backwash, i.e. by painting over a lighter colour such as yellow.

The one problem with ladder lettering is that mistakes are usually difficult to correct. If the unthinkable happens, write the correct letter over the top.

Partial lettering can be used with younger children who are not used to upper-case writing. It is more compact than ladder lettering, and can provide variety. Part of the letter is painted in

41

beforehand, and the rest is painted in during the message.

abcdefghijklmn
opqrstuvwxyz

Make sure that the letters are correctly spaced and that the words painted are not obvious in their uncompleted form.

Hidden lettering is written before a presentation using a white candle. Water-based paints will not stick to the wax, and so the letters can be revealed by brushing over them during the presentation using a dark-coloured paint.

Pictures

The cross is the most common symbol used in sketchboard talks. It can be painted in various ways, as shown below. The hill is often included as this can draw attention to the cross.

If the cross is painted up in several stages, various points can be made. If the cross bar is painted in first, the barrier caused by sin can be explained. Alternatively mathematical symbols can be used.

If the upright is painted in first the I in sin can be emphasised. If three crosses are painted in, the reactions of the two thieves can be used.

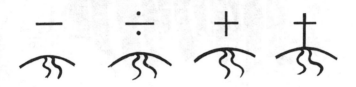

Stick men are often useful in stories.

A crowd can be drawn without such attention to detail.

Trees can also be painted quickly.

Some children's stories use landscapes or sea-scapes. In these pictures it is important to remember perspective. All the lines which point "in" to the board should converge on a common point in space known as the "vanishing point". This is especially important in the case of buildings. Outlines should be drawn in black, and should be as thin as possible.

Finally, keep paintings simple, especially if your artistic talent is limited, using bright colours and bold shapes.

Part III:
Reaching adults in the open air

9: An overview

There are many different types of Christian activity which are sometimes described as open-air evangelism. This handbook concentrates on proclamation using a sketchboard, which has been found to be an effective and transferable form of ministry in a wide number of situations around the world. It is recognised that open-air services, praise marches, open-air worship meetings, literature distribution and Christian art festivals can all be used by God, but as other publications already deal with these activities they will not be discussed here.

Adult meetings may take place in shopping centres, high streets, beaches, promenades or anywhere else that people gather. The central feature of such meetings will usually be the proclamation of the Gospel using a sketchboard. The preacher will paint up part of the message before starting to speak, and this will usually build a crowd. The preacher will then present the Christian message in an exciting and challenging way. Other Christians will stand around and form part of the gathering crowd. At the end of the message the preacher will ask people to respond, after which the team members will start conversations with those who have listened.

Sometimes the sketchboard message will be preceded by other items. Music can be used to build a crowd while the preacher is preparing the sketchboard. Drama can present a simple truth in a powerful way, while a testimony can prepare the crowd for the sketchboard message. Conjuring may be used to illustrate a particular point during the course of the message. However, it must be remembered that proclamation followed by personal contact are the key elements in effective evangelism, and that often the sketchboard preacher is in the best position to present the Gospel and prepare the crowd for counselling.

10: Choosing a site

There are two basic questions to ask when choosing an open-air site: "where do people gather?" and "where will they listen?" Choosing a good open-air site is not easy, but some effort at this stage can avoid a lot of wasted time later on. There are many factors to consider, and a site that was successful five years ago may be unsuitable now. It is a good idea to visit the area before organising an open air, if at all possible.

The best way to decide on a site is to watch where people go and what they do. Ideally a site should be chosen where a lot of people are wandering with plenty of time to listen. Bear in mind that the time of day will be crucial: a shopping centre that is crowded at midday on a Saturday may be empty on a Sunday evening. It is easiest to illustrate this with examples.

Places where people shop are often suitable for open-airs. The place with the most people may not always be the best place for a meeting. Some shops attract people who are in a hurry, whereas others encourage browsing. Crowds may be found around fast-food outlets, bus stations or taxi ranks. Covered arcades can be good, but many are private

and so require permission from the owners. Avoid places that are too noisy.

Railway and underground stations are very busy, especially during rush hours. Short programmes are preferable, because people normally travel to get somewhere! Gospel conjuring or a short piece of drama followed by the distribution of invitations may be more successful than a sketchboard message.

Beaches attract big crowds in the summer, but most of the people will be more interested in sleeping or swimming than in listening to a challenging message. The potential audience will also be dispersed along the beach, and there will be many distractions. However promenades or beach shops can be more successful. One advantage of the beach is that below mean high water mark local bye-laws do not apply, so if it is not possible to work on

the promenade, the sketchboard could be placed on the beach facing towards the passers-by.

Markets are often busy, noisy and full of stall-holders who will resent any competition for the attention of passers-by. However, exits from markets can sometimes be good open-air sites.

Examples of sites which are usually worth avoiding include bandstands, the centre of large squares and car parks. Although these places offer lots of space, they do not provide the intimate atmosphere or the throughflow of people necessary for consistently successful open airs.

One question raised by these examples is whether the easiest site should always be chosen. The answer will depend on the overall strategy guiding the evangelism. Sometimes open airs in a difficult area may be the only feasible way of reaching that area, but if an alternative exists it should be considered. It is also worth remembering that

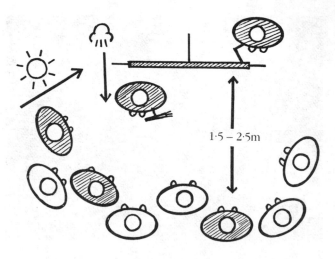

1·5 – 2·5m

work in a difficult area can be very demoralising for the team. On the other hand, a persistent witness in a tough area can sometimes win the respect of the residents in a way that nothing else will.

In ideal weather conditions the sketchboard should be placed at a slight angle to the sun (in the light but avoiding dazzling the preacher or crowd) and with the wind behind (to carry the preacher's voice). Obviously, some compromise will usually be necessary. In addition to the preacher, one team member will be required to hold the sketchboard. This may seem a mundane task, but a sudden gust of wind can wreck a meeting, especially if the falling board hits members of the crowd!

11: The role of team members

Introduction

The team members are as vital to an open-air programme as the preacher. Team members form the initial crowd, provide prayer support for the preacher and re-apply the message to individuals at the end of the preaching.

Any Christian can act as a team member. In fact a range of members of different age, sex and background will be best able to cope with the variety of people who will be contacted on the street. It is clearly essential that all team members are committed Christians.

Evangelism is pointless unless God directs and uses it (see chapter 1), and so prayer is an important part of the team member's role. Each person should have spent time praying before the meeting. The team should also meet together to pray, preferably immediately before the open-airs. During the meeting team members should pray both for the preacher and for those around him. After the meeting those not involved in counselling should pray for any conversations which are taking place.

It is important that a team leader, who may or may not be the preacher, is appointed, and that team members do what is asked of them. The street is the place for doing evangelism, not for discussing strategy!

The team should stand about 1.5–2.5m (4.5–7.5 feet) in front of the board, facing towards it. If the team is large (say more than eight) some of the team can stand further away and move in as the preaching begins. As preaching continues the team should spread themselves through the crowd in a non-conspicuous manner, thus making personal contact easier at the end of the meeting.

The preacher will end the message with an invitation (see chapter 15). The first priority of the team should be to talk to those who respond to the invitation, followed by those who have stayed to the end of the meeting. In exceptional circumstances team members may follow those who leave after the Gospel but before the invitation, but only if the team is large and it is possible to leave the meeting without causing a distraction.

It is easier to start conversations after a meeting than might be expected, because those who have listened to the message and stayed will usually be interested in spiritual things. Identify yourself and ask open questions (ie questions which don't have a "yes/no" answer). A good starting sentence is "Hello! I'm with the person who was just speaking. What did you think of what (s)he was saying?"

The role of team members

Do's and don'ts

DO smile at the preacher: it can be really lonely sometimes!

DO look interested, even if you have heard the message fifty times before. This will encourage others to pay attention.

DO stand close to the preacher during the message.

DO pray continally.

DO be prepared to give your testimony if called upon by the preacher.

DO carry a small Bible, some literature, and a pencil and paper to make a note of your contact's name and address.

DO look clean and reasonably tidy.

DO take literature for your use before or after the meeting.

DON'T walk off, especially in the middle of a meeting. If you *have* to leave, always tell the team leader where you are going.

DON'T argue with hecklers. Leave them to the preacher.

DON'T talk during the message. If someone in the crowd asks a question, give a polite but brief reply, promising to talk after the meeting.

DON'T distribute literature to the crowd during the meeting: it will destroy their concentration.

DON'T wear sunglasses if you can avoid it, especially the mirror type: it is hard to talk to someone without establishing eye contact.

DON'T take the literature offered by the preacher or respond to the invitation. This will confuse the crowd when they realise that you and the preacher are working together.

12: Counselling

At the end of an open-air meeting team members will begin to counsel those who have taken literature or who have listened to most of the message. It is at this point that the truths discussed during the presentation can be explained in detail to individuals.

Starting a conversation

If someone has listened to much of an open-air meeting, they will probably be fairly interested in what is being said. Ask a good opening question which identifies you with the speaker and which requires more than a yes/no answer. An example sentence is given in the previous chapter.

Try to find out as much as you can about the contact without being intrusive. It is then easier to choose subjects which are relevant for the contact, and it shows that you consider them to be more than "pew fodder". For example, ask about previous contact with churches, beliefs about God and things in the message which were hard to accept. Do not talk up to or down to your contact.

Presenting the Gospel

Once you have listened to the contact for a few minutes, look for an opportunity to present your testimony in a natural way. Then ask if you can tell the contact how to have a personal relationship with God. Present the Gospel in brief, simple but complete form. Many people find that it is useful to use the literature offered by the preacher as the basis for this Gospel presentation. The leaflet can keep the conversation on track, and shows the contact that the presentation will not continue indefinitely! Afterwards the contact keeps the literature as a reminder of the conversation. However the leaflet must never become a script, and sometimes it may be better to adopt, a freer approach. Ask God to give you discernment in applying his word to peoples' lives (Heb 4:12).

Once the Gospel has been explained, ask if it makes sense. Don't be surprised if you have to explain the same point several times. If the contact accepts the Gospel, ask him if he is ready to make Christ Lord of his life. Explain both the costs and the benefits of becoming a Christian.

If your contact wants to become a Christian, lead him in a prayer. Try to pray with your contacts, even if they do not want to respond to the Gospel, believing that the Holy Spirit will convict them of their sin. Leave them with some literature, or challenge them to read through John's Gospel.

Do's and don'ts

DO be kind and loving. How you say things is as important as what you say.
DO be familiar with the literature that is being used.
DO be open to God while you counsel.
DO direct the conversation towards Christ.

DON'T hesitate to start the conversation.
DON'T interrupt other people's conversations.
DON'T eat garlic or drink alcohol before an open air.
DON'T argue. If you are getting nowhere, share your testimony and end the discussion politely but firmly. Always try to part as friends.
DON'T use jargon. Words like "sin", "Christian" and "heaven" need explaining. Avoid words and phrases like "atonement", "penal subsitution", "saved", "redeemed", "sanctified", "Jesus in my heart", and "washed in the blood".
DON'T apologise for the Gospel. If people do not like it, that is their problem and not yours.

DON'T confuse "the offence of the cross" with the offence of your personality or attitude.
DON'T pressurise. If the Holy Spirit is working in a person's life he will convict in his own time.

13: Using a testimony

What is a testimony?

A testimony is a factual account a witness gives of events he has seen. For example, someone observing a murder or a car accident might be called by a court to describe what he saw. A Christian's testimony is an account of the workings of God in his life before, during and after his conversion. It is not based on opinions but on experience.

We cannot help being witnesses as we have all seen God at work in our lives. However, it is possible to be a bad witness by not reporting what we have seen, distorting events, or drawing attention to ourselves instead of God. Instead, we need to be good and faithful witnesses. As 1 Peter 3:15 says, "Always be prepared to give an answer to everyone who asks you to give the reason for the hope that you have".

Why use your testimony?

Many Christians think that their testimony is of little interest and not worth telling. Not all testimonies involve spectacular changes from wicked sinners to perfect saints, but then most contacts will be with fairly unspectacular people. An ordinary testimony may mean more to ordinary people than an x-rated epic! The Bible contains the testimonies of people from all walks of life: religious leaders (Acts 22); notorious sinners (John 4); and even former demoniacs (Mark 5:20).

A testimony is a very effective and useful tool. Some people are capable of arguing on doctrinal or philosophical matters forever, but they will find it very hard to contradict your personal experience of God. One major difference between Christianity and other religions is that Christians have a living relationship with God, and your testimony can help to explain this more clearly. Most people are interested in personal stories, and so your testimony will also encourage your contact to enquire further about your faith. The best way to prepare your testimony is to spend some time thinking about your experience of God and writing it down.

Writing your testimony

Your testimony should consist of three main elements: Before Conversion (BC), During Conversion (DC) and After Conversion (AC). These elements can be seen in the testimony of Paul before Festus and Agrippa (Acts 26:4–23).

In the first section (Before Conversion) talk about your life before you became a Christian (cf Acts 26:4–11). This section should be brief and deal with specific things in your life that were missing or things that were wrong. Try to choose things with which the person listening can identify, but do not distort the truth. Avoid making your sin seem attractive.

In the "During Conversion" section (cf Acts 26:12–18) try to explain what happened, giving as much relevant detail as possible. Avoid jargon and do not slip into a twenty minute Gospel message.

In the "After Conversion" section of the testimony (cf Acts 26:19–23) it is important to show how your life has changed for the better since becoming a Christian. Concentrate on specific things you have mentioned earlier and show how those things have changed. Remember to be positive; emphasising all the "enjoyable" things which you do not do anymore will not commend the Gospel to others.

You should aim to be able to give your testimony in three minutes, with one minute for each element. Once you have mastered this, you will find it easy to speak for longer when required.

If you have listened to the person earlier, you will have some idea of what he is looking for in life, and hopefully will be able to find something in your own testimony that he will relate to. Thus on different occasions your testimony will emphasise different aspects of what God has done for you. Some things to consider include: finding love and friendship that were missing before; forgiveness and release from guilt and anxiety; a new perspective and purpose in life; peace; joy; freedom from the fear of death. It is always good to mention that you are sure of going to heaven when you die; because many people are looking for this assurance.

If writing your testimony seems difficult because you were very young when you became a Christian or because you cannot remember the details, it is still possible to give a testimony. You can say that you came to an awareness of a need for God in your life and can show examples of God at work in you now.

Do's and don'ts

DO identify with your contact.
DO use humour constructively, particularly to relieve tension.
DO use personal examples and experiences, so your listener can visualise the situation.
DO be specific and follow ideas through.
DO be clear, honest and relaxed.
DO use your testimony regularly.
DO keep it short!

DON'T use clichés or religious jargon.
DON'T include irrelevant detail.
DON'T have a frivolous attitude to the Gospel.
DON'T emphasise negative aspects or dwell on failure.
DON'T jump from point to point or repeat yourself.
DON'T attack your family, friends or church.

14: Preparing and presenting a message

Preparation

The time spent in preparation for an open-air message is vital. In response to this suggestion some cite the command of Jesus not to worry what to say (eg Luke 21:14). However, this command is given in the context of an unjust trial in the midst of persecution, and its relevance to evangelism is unclear. It is true that some preachers have occasionally produced powerful messages on the spur of the moment, and no amount of study will compensate for a lack of some natural ability or the absence of God's empowering, but as a rule the quality of a message will depend on the quality of the preparation.

Some beginners prefer to start with someone else's message. There is nothing at all wrong with this, and even Jesus began his ministry on the same theme as his predecessor John the Baptist (cf Matt 3:2 and Matt 4:17). An advantage of starting with a tried and tested message is that the basic structure will be sound. However the preacher must make each message his own, and this will usually require a considerable amount of work.

Pray that God will guide you as you prepare. A good preacher will be sensitive to the questions, issues and trends in his society, and to what God is wanting to say in response. The guidelines for messages that are given here should not be ignored lightly, but neither should they be seen as sacred laws.

A good place to start is by choosing a subject. Look for something which is interesting (both to you and the intended audience), and which will provide good lead-ins to the Gospel. Jesus chose subjects from everyday life (eg Matt 13:3,47;18:12), and Paul often started his addresses from the viewpoint of the listeners (Acts 17:22–23). Avoid subjects which are overtly religious, as well as negative subjects. If you want to tackle an issue such as *aids* or *war*, it is better to start from a positive angle (for example *health* or *peace*). Generally speaking, people will stop more easily to listen to something which they think will be enjoyable, and the Gospel is after all primarily Good News.

Once you have decided on a subject, make lists of as many positive and negative words as possible which relate to this subject. For example, if the message was to be about love, positive words might include "accepted", "worth", "trust", "secure" and "friend". The negative list might contain such words as "hate", "betrayed", "lust", "hurt" and "fear".

By now you should be starting to have some ideas about the content of your message. As you look down the list some of the words will seem

67

difficult to talk about. Others will be too long to use on a sketchboard (for example the word "environment" will take practically the whole width of the sketchboard). Try to choose a negative word that shows a problem with respect to the subject, and another negative word which shows the result of this problem. Similarly, look for a positive word which describes the solution to the problem that you have identified and another word which denotes the result of accepting this solution. The diagram below should make this clearer. Then look for a catchy title to summarise your subject.

A tendency of most inexperienced preachers is to give two messages one after the other. The first will be on an interesting subject, will have no spiritual content and will last much longer than the second, which will be an extremely compressed Gospel message. To avoid this trap it is important to work out how to introduce Christian content throughout the message. The use of appropriate Bible verses can be helpful (obviously, these should be taken from a modern translation, and the reference should not be given). In the structure shown below the first negative word is used to encourage the *recognition* of sin, while the second is used to explain the *result* of sin. After this, the cross is painted up and God's *remedy* for sin is explained. The next word is used to teach the need for *repentance* from sin. Finally the second positive word shows one promise which is ours when we are *released* from sin.

At the end of the message there will normally be an invitation, which is dealt with in chapter 15. If the Gospel has been preached properly the

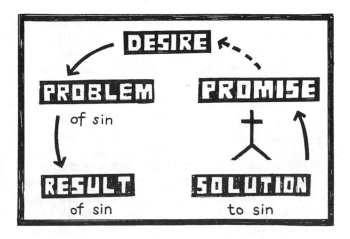

invitation should flow naturally from the message, and if this is not the case it may be a sign that some more work is needed.

The layout of the board is largely a matter of taste, but nonetheless there are some advantages in following the form illustrated in this chapter. The title should appear at the top of the board, negative words should be listed down the lefthand side and positive words should appear on the right together with the cross. There is some consensus that colours such as red carry positive connotations while darker colours such as blue and black are associated with negative ideas, so this is often reflected in the colours chosen for different words, though once again it is possible to become too conscious of such considerations: red can also represent negative concepts such as danger, while black can sometimes represent positive concepts such as excellence or value (for example a black belt in Judo or the black ball in snooker).

It is useful to write out the message, or at least to jot down the board layout, the main ideas and the link between words. Also, make a note of any other ideas which occur to you for other messages.

Presentation

Pray before, during and after your presentation. Open-air preaching is a spiritual event, and as such it involves the preacher in spiritual battle. Expect to use the material that you have prepared, but be ready to change it. There is little point in presenting a message about world politics and the spread of materialism if your crowd consists entirely of 12 year-olds!

Do not shout. Shouting distorts your face and gives the impression that you are a fanatic. It also means that people have no reason to approach the board, and so your crowd will remain spread over a large area. Project your voice and invite people to draw closer. This will create a more intimate atmosphere, which will help to keep your audience until the end of the message.

Try to develop a rapport with your crowd. While it is hard to explain how this is done, it is easy to know when you have achieved it! Establish eye contact with individuals, but do not stare. Ask questions and expect an answer. Even simple requests like "please move forward" can help. Remember to talk to your crowd rather than to the sketchboard, the paintbox or the treetops.

Always paint up your next keyword before men-

tioning it. This takes some practice. Prepare some standard ways of introducing a keyword which do not include the world itself. For example, "Other people try this way" or "The real problem in this".

If the worst happens and you make a mistake with the painting or lose your train of thought, take a deep breath and pick up the message from the next keyword. Morbid introspection is not a good basis for social events, and launching into a monologue along the lines of "Oh no, now I've made a mistake. I always do this when I'm nervous. I really am terribly sorry. Why am I so stupid. . ." will help to disperse your crowd in record time. Bear in mind that at least some of the crowd will be amazed that you have the courage to stand up and speak in public at all, and that the rest may be encouraged to watch the rest of the meeting if for no other reason than to see you make more mistakes!

71

Hecklers are rare, and if handled properly can actually build a crowd. In general, ignore them, and they will soon become bored. If they persist, remind them that it is your meeting and promise to speak to them at the end. Be polite and you will gain the respect of those watching.

When you come to the end of your message, stop! It is always tempting to recap, especially if no-one responds to the message, but the team will usually be in a better position than you to deal with individuals who have questions. A good length to aim for is ten minutes, although a good fifteen-minute presentation will hold the crowd better, and seem shorter, than a five-minute message that has been badly prepared or poorly delivered.

15: The invitation

Jesus called his first disciples to follow him publicly (eg Mark 1:16–18, 2:13–14, 3:13) and expects us to do the same today. Repentance is not an option in God's eyes (Acts 17:30). Often there is a big difference between knowing something in theory and being ready to act on that knowledge in practice. Giving an invitation at the end of a message ensures that those listening realise that believing the Gospel has consequences. It also gives an opportunity for people to respond publicly to the Gospel, and those who do not respond know that there was a step which they did not take.

It has already been mentioned that the invitation should be an integral part of the message. As ambassadors for Christ we should act "as though God were making his appeal through us" (2 Cor 5:20), and this desire for people to respond to God's initiative towards mankind should always be present in our preaching.

By the time the invitation is reached the Gospel should have been explained. It is important to spell out the cost of following Christ, but also the benefits of doing so and the danger in rejecting him. When Peter counselled those in Jerusalem he both warned them and pleaded with them (Acts 2:40).

The most common form of invitation is made using a piece of literature. The evangelist will hold a leaflet at arm's length and say something like "You can show your willingness to follow Jesus for the first time today by stepping forward and taking one of these leaflets from my hand". The leaflet should then be passed slowly in front of the crowd, giving them time to respond. After a suitable period the evangelist can close the meeting so that counselling can begin.

Sometimes it is inappropriate to use literature. For example, in some countries where printed matter is rare, the offer of free literature can provoke a near riot. In this case it may be more appropriate to invite people to shake hands with the preacher.

16: Follow-up

It is not always possible to arrange follow-up for contacts made on the street, but, nevertheless, follow-up should be a high priority. Some of the most bitter critics of Christianity are people who made some kind of decision but who were never followed up. Often this follow-up will have to be handled by someone other than the person who led the contact to Christ, but it is still the responsibility of those involved in evangelism to ensure that follow-up occurs.

This chapter will give only an outline of the requirements in follow-up work. There are already many good books about follow-up, and in any case there is insufficient space in this handbook to do justice to such an important subject. Possible sources of further information are given in the reading list.

The most immediate need of someone who has just made a decision is for counselling on assurance. New Christians often experience all sorts of doubts and fears in the days following their conversion, and so it is well worth spending a few minutes showing them a few of the many verses in the Bible which point to the security of salvation through

Christ (eg Heb 13:5, 1 John 5:11–13). Evangelistic leaflets often include a section on assurance.

The basics of the Christian life such as prayer, Bible study and corporate worship will need to be dealt with. Obviously, learning to practice such basics is a lifelong process, and while the importance of regular devotions must be stressed, this must not be done in such a way as to load the new Christian with feelings of inadequacy or guilt.

The command to be a witness should be explained. Often new Christians are the most effective evangelists, and in any case it is never too early to start developing good habits. One way of verifying the reality of a decision made on the street is to ask the convert to explain that decision to a different team member: this has the added advantage of tackling the hurdle of the first testimony.

In the rush to explain all the things that need to be learned it should not be forgotten that Christianity is about a personal relationship with God. It will be encouraging to explain that the Holy Spirit will comfort, strengthen, guide and equip the new Christian.

In the mid to long term, integration into a local church is vital. The gap between the Church and the world is cultural as well as spiritual, and so this process may not be without its problems. Nurture Groups (small groups of new Christians who study basic Christian beliefs with a leader) can smooth this process. In some cases a one-to-one discipleship programme with a mature Christian may be more appropriate.

None of the excellent follow-up materials available are any substitute for the investment of time and love in the new Christian's life. The example of other Christians will have a powerful effect, and so those involved in evangelism and follow-up need to be wary of negating their words by their actions. In particular, evangelists should avoid the temptation to drop all interest in a contact as soon as he is saved in order to go in search of the next convert.

Part IV:
Reaching children in the open air

17: An overview

Why bother with children?

Child evangelism in the open air is an important but often neglected means to fulfil the Great Commission. Children need the Gospel as much as anyone else (Rom 3:23), and a high percentage of Christians in churches today made a commitment to Christ at an early age. Many great men and women of God were converted as children, for example:–

Catherine Booth (Salvation Army leader) was 6.
Jonathan Edwards (preacher) was 8.
Matthew Henry (Bible commentator) was 11.
Graham Kendrick (singer, songwriter) was 6.
Graham Scroggie (preacher, teacher) was 9.
Mary Slessor (missionary to Africa) was 7.
Bishop Taylor Smith (Chaplain General of the Armed Forces) was 11.
Count Zinzendorf (founder of the Moravian Missionary society) was 4.

The potential of a young life given to Christ, and therefore of a whole lifetime available to serve God, is huge. Jesus considered that children were worth

spending time with (eg Mark 10:13–14), and we would do well to follow his example.

Organisation of children's meetings

Children's meetings often take place in parks or on ground near to housing estates, as well as at holiday locations such as beaches. The children are encouraged to sit on a plastic sheet or stand behind a rope, and the Gospel is then presented through games, songs, quizzes, memory verses and a sketchboard message, which is usually based on a Bible story. Children who want to know more talk to team members who will carefully explain the Gospel.

As well as presenting the Gospel to children, these meetings can provide a point of contact with whole families. Parents who would not stop at an adult open-air meeting or talk on their doorstep will often watch a children's programme, and team members may then be able to present the Gospel to them.

18: Choosing a site

There are several requirements of a good site for children's work

Firstly, there should be children around! This may sound obvious, but just because a council has erected a playground in a certain place it does not mean that children ever use it. The time of the meeting will affect the choice of a site. For example, there are some areas where children only seem to play between the end of school and tea-time. Housing estates are usually promising, especially if there are blocks of flats. Beaches may also be worth trying, especially in the afternoon, when the children have exhausted all the other sources of entertainment.

Secondly, the site should be safe. Stay away from swings and other playground equipment that is likely to jettison flying children at short notice. Footballs can be equally hazardous, so avoid areas of grass used for ball games. Remember that if your site is close to a main road you may inadvertently encourage children to cross this road in order to reach your meetings.

Thirdly, the site should be visible. This will encourage other children to join the meetings as

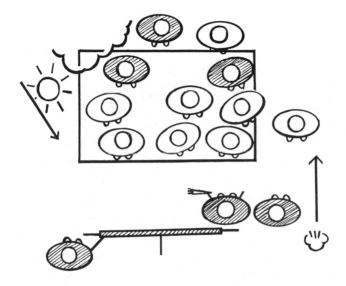

well as reassuring anxious parents that you have nothing to hide.

Fourthly, you should choose a site that will be comfortable for the children. Flat, dry, grassy sites are often best. If the ground is dusty or damp, a plastic sheet should help to keep clothes clean and parents happy.

Set up the meeting so that the children have their backs to the sun and with the sketchboard at an angle to it: this will reduce glare. If there is any wind try to set up so that it is blowing towards the audience.

19: The role of team members

A children's programme will often involve several different activities, and also, ideally, a number of team memers who will be involved in the presentation (see chapter 21). Presenting a quiz or a memory verse can be a gentle introduction to sketchboard work, and using several different team members provides variety for the children.

The children will be asked to sit on a plastic sheet or stand behind a rope, and most team members should mingle with them. They should join in with singing, actions etc. to encourage the children, and can also help to control children during the meeting. A few team members should stand around the meeting, to prevent interference from older children and to talk to parents who want to know about the meeeting. Sometimes it can be useful for a few people to walk around the area where the meeting is being held and invite other children to join in.

Do's and don'ts

DO be amusing: keep the children happy but don't over-excite them.

DO be approachable: be prepared to talk to the children and make friends with them.

DO be enthusiastic: enjoy yourself and throw yourself into the activities. Children can tell if you are embarrassed.

DO be aware of possible problems from older children, and concern from parents. If parents are present, consult them before giving their children literature.

DO be tidy: What to you is an open-air site may be someone else's home.

DO be prepared to counsel children.

DO be firm but loving to any troublemakers.

NEVER, NEVER touch the children, or lead them away from the meeting. Parents are rightly concerned for the safety of their children, and a misunderstanding can severely damage the reputation of the church or organisation involved in the open air.

20: Counselling

Perhaps the most essential point to bear in mind when counselling children is not to push them towards a decision. Children love to please, and can be persuaded to say all kinds of things in order to satisfy a friendly adult. The key to counselling children is to let them take the initiative in responding to the Gospel. Do not be afraid to send away children who are not sure that they want to become Christians, ideally with some literature.

The main steps involved in counselling a child are shown by the diagram below. The four questions in diamond-shaped boxes show the paths that a conversation may take. These questions are for the counsellor rather than the child, and need not necessarily be asked as such.

Start by making friends, finding out the child's name and talking generally about the programme. Then try to ascertain why the child has come to talk to you. There may be many reasons apart from the one you are hoping for. If the child is unsure or says something general (for example that he enjoyed the programme) recap on the message of the meeting and let the child leave to think things over. Sometimes the child will just want to ask questions or play a game, in which case be prepared

Open-Air Evangelism

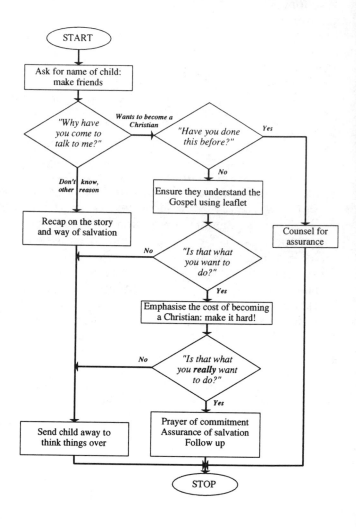

START

Ask for name of child: make friends

"Why have you come to talk to me?"

Wants to become a Christian

Don't know, other reason

"Have you done this before?"

Yes

No

Recap on the story and way of salvation

Ensure they understand the Gospel using leaflet

Counsel for assurance

No

"Is that what you want to do?"

Yes

Emphasise the cost of becoming a Christian: make it hard!

No

"Is that what you **really** want to do?"

Yes

Send child away to think things over

Prayer of commitment
Assurance of salvation
Follow up

STOP

to demonstrate your interest in the child in a practical way.

When a child says that he wants to become a Christian, ask him if he has ever done so before. It is possible that the child has already made a decision but is lacking in assurance or wants to be certain of forgiveness for a sin committed since his conversion. Suggesting that he "prays again" will only confuse him further.

Assuming that the child does want to become a Christian and hasn't done so before, ensure that he understands the Gospel. Avoid questions with yes/no answers in favour of open questions that will encourage the child to talk. You may need to cover the same points several times. If the child loses interest during the explanation be ready to drop the subject.

Once you are satisfied that the child understands the Gospel it is safe to ask him what he wants to do. If the answer is still that he wants to become a Christian, explain the consequences, emphasising that the decision is for always and that sometimes it will be hard. Then ask him again! This process may seem laborious, but at least you will be able to have confidence in any decision that is finally made. If the child hesitates at any stage, suggest that he thinks about it a bit more and talk about something different.

If after all the above the child still wants to become a Christian, lead him through a prayer, if possible using the literature. Then counsel for assurance, which may include re-explaining the Gospel to show that it really works for him, now. Ask the child to explain the decision he has taken to another team member as a further check that the message has been grasped. Organise follow-up (see chapter 24).

Do's and don'ts

DO sift out true inquirers.
DO ask open questions.
DO be careful with literature: if the parents are around ask their permission before giving leaflets to their children.
DO keep everything simple.
DO use the Word of God in counselling . . . but not too many verses and watch the version.
DO try to encourage the child to explain in his own words what he wants to ask you.

DON'T take it for granted that he understands . . . ask him to explain each step in his own words.
DON'T try to pull unripe fruit from the tree.
DON'T be afraid to show your excitement when a child is converted.
DON'T forget to organise follow-up.

21: Running a children's meeting

There is no one way of running a children's meeting. The ideas described here have been found to work in a variety of situations, but there is plenty of scope for experimentation, remembering that the main aim of a children's meeting is not to entertain, but to present spiritual ideas and to introduce children to Jesus.

On arriving at the chosen site, the children's attention must be attracted, as they may not be expecting anything interesting to be happening. Attention can be attracted in a variety of ways, one of the most effective being music. Singing or musical instruments can be used on initial entry to the site, or a tour of the site can be made, making as much noise as possible (within reason). Another possibility is to have some team members wandering around the site, letting the children know that the meeting is about to start. Using a puppet and ventriloquism can be helpful.

Once a group of children have gathered, the meeting can begin. Sometimes it is worth starting the meeting, even when no children have been found, as the meeting itself can attract children.

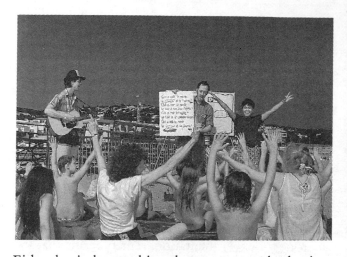

Either begin by teaching them a song or by having a sketch time (see the resources sections). This will keep them guessing and entertain them. Usually there is little spiritual content at this point, the aim being to make friends.

The next part of the programme is often a quiz time. This can combine secular and spiritual questions. Choose a game that is familiar to the children and that can be easily represented on the board, such as noughts and crosses, snakes and ladders or blockbusters (some examples of all these ideas are given in the resources sections). The questions must be answered before the child is allowed to throw the dice or decide where to put his mark. Start with simple questions about things that interest the children, and include some general knowledge and biblical questions later. This enables you to start introducing spiritual ideas and to find out how much Bible knowledge the children have. It is wise to have a mixture of relatively easy and difficult questions. It may help to try out some questions first on children you know to help you to decide upon the right level, remembering that, unfortunately, Sunday school children are not typical of those you will meet on the street. Sometimes the quiz can be used after the story to see if the children remember what happened and to reinforce the teaching.

The next part of the programme is usually the scripture memory verse. Again it is important to present this in an interesting way. For example, play a form of hang-man, where the children are given blanks instead of words and they have to guess the letters to discover the verse. If they guess a letter correctly it is written in every time it occurs in the verse, while if they guess wrongly they lose one more chance (see chapter 34). The aim is for the children to win every time. When the whole text has been revealed, the children can be asked to repeat it in a variety of ways: quietly and loudly; quickly and slowly; standing and sitting etc. To make this task more difficult some of the words can be rubbed out, helping them to memorise the text. Remember to give the Bible reference with the text.

The final part of the programme is the story, usually chosen from the Bible. This is usually between seven and fifteen minutes long. The story needs to be applied continually to the children as well as being interesting (see the next chapter).

When planning a programme, a theme needs to be chosen. This theme provides continuity and helps the children to retain what you have been talking about. The programme should also include relevant Bible verses and quiz questions, put together in a varied and lively way. All the items should flow together naturally and be presented on a bright and colourfully painted board. A meeting should last around 45 minutes.

Sometimes it will be possible to work with the same children on a number of occasions. In this case the theme can be continued across more than one meeting, although each meeting must also make sense in isolation. If you are doing a series of meetings with the same children, you could offer a prize at the end for anyone who can remember all the memory verses you have taught them.

22: Preparing and presenting a story

When planning a children's message it is important to keep things simple. Each point should be clear and easily understood. This can be achieved by explaining, illustrating and applying every point as it is made. It is also essential to make the message interesting or you will lose your audience. If there is a wide age range to contend with, aim the message at those in the middle, and apply the points at different levels.

There are three main points that need to be covered. The first is the idea of sin, what it is and its consequences. Then there is the remedy for sin, explaining the point of Jesus' death and resurrection. Finally there is the need to make a personal decision to follow Christ. (See chapter 3 for a fuller outline of the Gospel.) Ideally all these points should be covered in a single message, but if the story is part of a programme spanning several days it is possible to emphasise different points on different days.

Preparation

Before selecting a story it is important to pray for guidance. Then select a story that makes a good point, that appeals to you, and that you feel you can retell comfortably. The stories of Jesus are ideal, and some Old Testament stories can also be useful. Look for points raised by the story which can be applied to the children's lives. Spend time thinking about the story, the setting, and about how the characters would have felt. Get to know the story, read it in different translations, look it up in commentaries and try to understand what it is about. When you feel you know the story, write it out in your own words, including all the applications and everything that you want to say. You may not eventually present the story as you have written it, but this exercise will help to crystallise your thoughts.

The best way of improving a story is to practise it. As you tell the story you will gain new insights and inspiration. Finally, keep a record of the story for future use, by yourself or by others.

Telling the story

If you make the start of the story interesting, you will be more likely to retain the children's interest. Developing a rapport with the children and encouraging them to join in is also important. Use actions, gestures and body-language to tell the story. The introduction should set the scene and give a clue about the rest of the story. Avoid being vague, but do not give away the ending.

Events should follow in a logical order, with regular application of the Gospel to the children's own lives. The most common mistake made with children's stories is to leave all the application to the end. Look for things in the central character's life to introduce the idea of sin. Continue the action and suspense in the story, showing the struggle and conflict within the character. When you come to deal with the cross, explain clearly why Jesus died, perhaps using an analogy that children will understand.

You should always aim the message at the children, even if adults are present at the meeting. If you start to preach to the adults you are liable to forget the children and lose their interest and understanding, as well as missing the adults. Often adults will listen to a children's message precisely because it is *not* aimed at them!

23: The invitation

The aim of all evangelistic work among children should be to encourage boys and girls to respond willingly and sincerely to the claims of Jesus Christ as Lord and Saviour. An invitation is thus as relevant for children as for adults. However care must be exercised. The following points are worth noting:

A: Children must understand how Jesus can become their Saviour. They need to be shown what this will mean to them in the future.

B: The challenge must be adequate and fair, so that children realise the consequences of neglecting or rejecting Christ. But they should not be threatened with hellfire and brimstone. Children need to be loved into the Kingdom of God. Threatening or frightening presentations have been known to lead to sleeplessness and emotional problems. Such behaviour on the part of evangelists gives the Gospel and children's evangelism a bad name.

C: Avoid a highly emotional atmosphere. Often it is good to end a children's programme with a song or some other activity to break any tension created by the invitation. At all costs avoid an invitation that will cause a "follow the leader" response. Children who are interested should be spoken to individually to reduce the danger of peer pressure.

The most common form of invitation used with children in the open air requires the child to speak to a designated team member after the meeting. As a rule, suggest that boys talk to a man and girls talk to a woman. Make sure that the children know who these people are, but do not labour the point.

24: Follow-up

This is the greatest weakness of a lot of work among children. There are difficulties that will be encountered in arranging follow-up, but these problems should be overcome whenever possible

One difference between following up children and most adults is that the evangelist may find himself in conflict with the child's parents. Dealing with such difficulties requires a lot of wisdom, but precautions can be taken to reduce the risks. Never say or imply anything that is critical of the parents in the child's hearing. Instruct the child to tell his parents about the decision he has taken, and to show any literature to them. It may be useful to write a letter to the child and to say in the letter that he should show it to his parents.

The sooner contact can be established between the child and a recognised church or Sunday school the less problems are likely to occur. Parents will usually be much less fearful of a church than an unknown group of roaming evangelists!

In the shorter term there are steps that the evangelist can take to help the child to grow in Christ, even if a subsequent visit cannot be arranged. Ensure that the child has a Bible in a modern translation. Explain in simple terms about prayer, witness and the need to meet with other Christians. Impress on him that the Holy Spirit is with him to help him from now on.

Part V
Additional techniques

25: Music

Music can be used in many ways in the open air. This chapter is concerned with the use of music alongside other forms of open-air evangelism. As with all the other components of an open-air programme, some discipline is required to ensure that the overall effect is ordered and balanced.

Music in an open-air programme can have at least three major purposes. Firstly, it can attract people: musical sounds carry well in the open air, and are more distinctive at a distance than the spoken voice. Secondly, it can relax people: good music is enjoyable and is often a contrast to the drabness of normal street life. Thirdly, it can arouse spiritual interest: well-chosen songs with good words can communicate something of the Gospel.

Having seen that music can be effective in the open air, it must also be said that very unrealistic things are sometimes expected of open-air music groups. It is often said that singing good Christian songs at an open air is equivalent to preaching the Gospel. This view is particularly hard to sustain when it is considered that many choruses which are currently popular in churches are practically incomprehensible to someone who does not have a good working knowledge of evangelical jargon.

As with any activity in the open air, musical contributions must be good. Some churches are happy to send unrehearsed groups out to sing on the streets when they would never allow such a group to take part in a service. Musicians and vocalists should be talented and well-prepared. Allow time for tuning instruments, remembering the need to retune when leaving a warm building.

Continuity is vital in the open air, and so the order of songs should be prepared beforehand. The key signatures, number of repeats, musical introductions and other details of the arrangements should also be agreed. Once the musical contribution has begun, it should run without pauses or verbal explanations of each song. At the end the musicians should participate in the rest of the programme, although this may not be easy while guarding a musical instrument.

It is usually best to avoid P.A. systems, which

always complicate open-airs and may also break local bye-laws. If you *must* use amplification (for example because the site is excessively noisy or because electronic instruments are being used) attention should be paid to obtaining the optimal sound quality: poorly adjusted amplification systems are extremely wearing to listen to. A lot can be done without electrical assistance if the vocalists are trained to project their voices and the musicians use appropriate instruments (for example steel – rather than nylon-string guitars). Ensure that the sound output is balanced, and in particular that the voices are not drowned.

Try to avoid unimaginative arrangements. Variations to try include key changes, instrumental solos, vocal solos, harmonies and rounds. The visible appearance of the musicians is important. If all those participating can wear similar clothes it will add to the impression that the music has been prepared. The group should be compact, close to the other open-air activities and all members should face the crowd. Do not use music books or word sheets as these prevent eye-to-eye contact with the crowd. Remember to smile.

When choosing songs look for fairly upbeat tunes and accessible words. Avoid songs that are repetitive or which do not have much content. The "Make Way" books are a good place to start, although other books contain some suitable material. It is also worth considering songs from Christian albums, which may be more inventive than choruses and hymns and which are often intended for a non-Christian audience.

26: Drama

Drama has become more popular in Christian circles in recent years. This change must be attributed largely to the efforts of groups such as "Footprints" and "Riding Lights", whose performances have demonstrated the power of drama to communicate the Christian message. However the question to be addressed in the context of this handbook is whether drama can be used to good effect in the open air.

The answer is a qualified "yes". It is important to consider the goal of street drama, and therefore the type of presentation which will fulfil this goal. Taking a sketch that was intended for use in a church and expecting it to work in the open air is not the way to proceed.

The first requirement for a piece of street drama is that it carries a simple message. There are some excellent allegorical and satirical works available in the Christian press, but subtlety of this sort is wasted in the open air. The ever-changing audience, the numerous distractions, the difficulty of seeing and hearing every gesture and word and the atmosphere which often prevails on the street all contribute to this. In particular, mime is extremely difficult to do well in the open-air, although as

always there are exceptions. Choose a piece which will convey one simple point, which other items in the programme can expand on.

Secondly, street drama must cause people to think. Open-air work is not for the amusement of the crowd or the team, although often humour can be used to communicate a serious point. It is sometimes suggested that an enjoyable but content-free sketch will encourage people to stop, but unfortunately an expectation of "safe" entertainment is created within the listener which hinders rather than helps communication.

Thirdly, street drama must be accessible. All the comments in other chapters about appropriate language apply, but an added problem in the case of drama is that often the humour in published works assumes a knowledge of evangelical Christian subculture on the part of the audience, which will not be valid in the open air.

Fourthly, street drama must be foolproof. It is a fair assumption that anything that can go wrong will, and so the actors should know the piece sufficiently well to improvise if necessary. Avoid complex or fragile props for the same reason.

Fifthly, street drama must be integrated into the rest of the open-air programme. The actors must know when to start their presentation and how it will finish. The drama team should be ready to work as team members when they are not acting.

Finally, street drama must be of a high quality. Your potential audience will judge you in the light of what they see on television and in theatres. Comparison will also be made with the buskers and secular street actors who make their living by performing well. This requirement does not contradict with the first one of simplicity: simple drama can be performed well or badly.

When looking for suitable sketches, bear in mind that you may have to carry all the props to and from the open-air site, or wear the costumes for several hours. Avoid P.A. systems, because this will push the crowd away and annoy local residents, as well as further complicating the running of the open-air.

There are a number of good books on Christian drama, subject to the warnings given above, and some of these are named in the reading list. Alternatively you may wish to write your own sketches.

27: Conjuring

The definition of the word "conjuring" given in the Concise Oxford Dictionary is "to produce magical effects by natural means, perform marvels". Gospel conjuring involves the use of a particular class of visual aid (tricks) to present the Christian message.

Since conjuring is a specialist skill the techniques will not be covered in detail here. The reading list gives the addresses of organisations such as the Fellowship of Christian Magicians which organise training courses for those interested in learning more about conjuring. Local magician's shops may also be able to help. This chapter concentrates on one of the most important questions for Christian conjurers: how to use conjuring to communicate a spiritual truth.

As always, the visual aid should serve the preacher rather than the other way round. It is easy to become so fascinated by the techniques of conjuring that the spiritual application is forgotten or tagged on as an afterthought. Applications should flow naturally from the trick.

The time to start thinking about the application is before you buy the trick. Look for props which are big, bright and bold, and which can be used to illustrate a spiritual point. Tricks which involve colours can often be associated with a particular concept, such as scarlet for sin, green for envy, white for holiness or blue for heaven. If you do use colour in this way do not use the same colour for more than one concept in a programme, or you will confuse the audience.

Once you have a trick and a truth which needs communicating (other than to justify the purchase of the trick!) write down the script (or "patter"). The main point of the application should coincide with the climax of the trick. Then work back, looking for other points that can be made earlier in the patter. Remove all the waffle until the patter is "lean" and relevant. To perform Gospel conjuring successfully you will need to know both the patter and the trick inside out so that they become almost automatic.

The best tricks are often simple. Be content with one main point per trick. To preach a more complicated message either use a series of tricks, or use conjuring with another visual aid, such as the sketchboard. Look for all the points at which the trick can go wrong, and try to think of a suitable patter line which will cover you in case the worst happens.

Any form of evangelism should be well done, but the need for professionalism is perhaps more acute in conjuring than in any other area discussed in this handbook. To learn to deliver a trick with showmanship, precision and a good message can take hours of practice. If you are not prepared for this it is wiser to try a different means of communication. It is better to have one or two well-rehearsed tricks (as is the case for most open-air preachers) than to have a cupboard full of tricks which are inadequately prepared.

28: Escapology

Escapology may be considered to be a branch of conjuring, although often escapologists do not use conjuring routines and vice versa. The routines obviously centre on escape, be it from chains, ropes, sacks or cabinets.

There are several advantages in using escapology to present the Gospel. Escapology can draw large crowds in the open air, especially if the props are spectacular. The crowd will watch to see the escape (or perhaps see the escape fail!), and in the meantime the escapologist can preach the Gospel. If people start to leave, a few rattles of chains will keep them watching.

It does not matter if the audience is close to the escapologist or even surrounding him. There is often the possibility of audience participation which helps to build a rapport. There is a natural build-up to the preaching, ie being chained up, and this will mean the crowd will gather ready for the start of your presentation.

Escapology also has its disadvantages. The escapologist himself will often be too exhausted to speak to people afterwards, and the crowd will tend to disperse more quickly than normal, requiring rapid action on the part of the team members

to start conversations. All escapology tends to lead most naturally to applications about bondage and freedom, and so it is difficult to introduce much variety into the programme.

The effectiveness of an escapology routine depends to a large extent on the dramatic way in which it is presented: "Your presentation should be in the modern idiom, quick, slick, sensational. . .there is no other branch of magic which offers so much scope for flamboyant, dramatic showmanship."[8] Use large-linked chains because they look much more impressive, as well as being easier to escape from than the smaller sort.

Sources of further information are given in the reading list.

8. Escapes, Supreme Magic Company, 1979.

29: Ventriloquism

A small, dirty faced, fair headed girl runs up as an evangelist gets out of her car, "I know you, you're the puppet lady, is Horace in your car?" A knock at the door: it's Stephen, a thirteen year-old boy who often calls in asking if he can see Horace. Two good reasons for using a puppet in the open-air.

There can be no doubt that children relate to a puppet in an amazing way, and that therefore ventriloquism is an excellent means of communication. It crosses the boundaries of age, class, sex, religion and often even language! Using a puppet in another country, even when he needs a translator, proves just as popular as in Britain.

There are several reasons for making use of such a tool in a children's open-air meeting. Firstly, a ventriloquist's puppet, or any other puppet, is an excellent way of attracting children to a meeting. As you send out the team to collect children, inviting them to come to a meeting, the addition of a few puppets makes it obvious that the meeting will be fun. They immediately attract the children and make it easier for the team to speak to them.

The second advantage of using a puppet in the presentation is that he provides a bridge between the evangelist and the children. There is no logical

reason why children should want to sit and listen
to an unknown person telling a story, but if you
can produce a puppet and do something they will
really enjoy watching, you then have credibility!
The puppet is friends with whoever tells the story,
so the children can also be friends. If they enjoy

the ventriloquism routine, they get the idea that the rest of the programme will be good too. In a situation where the puppet is already known the attraction is even greater. As soon as the suitcase is in sight (puppets live in suitcases!) there is always the hope that he might come out. Sometimes he doesn't come out, which makes the next visit more exciting!

This leads to a third reason for using this tool, as a kind of incentive for good behaviour. This works in two ways; firstly, he will only come out of his case if the children are good enough to deserve him. This is not just a ploy on the part of a desperate evangelist, but a real necessity as it is impossible to produce an effective ventriloquism routine with a crowd of unruly youngsters, so if they are too unruly, the puppet stays in bed. Secondly, at the end of the routine, the puppet usually finds out that there is going to be a story. He may well have a few words with the story-teller, and of course he wants to listen. Now if he is to listen, the children will have to be quiet so he can hear, and by use of this device you can quieten a whole crowd of excited children ready for the story.

Finally, a ventriloquism routine can contribute greatly to the message we are presenting. Whatever the routine (and they are as endless as your imagination) they usually get around to the point that the puppet has a problem: he is often naughty and can't seem to be good for more than two minutes. He's tried everything and it hasn't worked. . ."well listen to the story and let's see if we can help you!" In fact the puppet can bring out whatever aspect

121

of the message you wish to emphasise, providing he is fun!

There are many ventriloquist's puppets available, depending on your preference and your purse, but many evangelists find the most useful type to be those in which your hand becomes the puppet's hand, thus giving endless scope for use of different props. There are one or two good books available about how to be a ventriloquist, and, in all honesty, anyone can do it with practice: all you need is to get started. It is great fun, and a fantastic communication tool.

The sample routine given in chapter 33 of this handbook would fit most children's programmes and could be fitted in just before the story. It's been tried and tested in schools and the open air, in Britain and in Southern Europe and it works well.

Part VI:
Resources

30: Sketchboard messages for adults

The following messages have been collected from many different sources. Many of them have evolved and been adapted over a long period, and so it is difficult to give credit to the original author. Apologies to anyone who has been overlooked!

"What do you follow" was written by Simon Ponsonby. It has been slightly adapted for inclusion in this handbook.

"Miami Vice" was written by Mark Detzler.

"True love" was developed at an OAC training seminar led by Paul Morley. The version here is by Mark Howe.

"What do you want?" was written by Caroline Pullen.

"Something beautiful" was written by Mark Howe, based on an idea by Korky Davey.

"Happiness" was written by Susan Howe.

"The whole truth" was written by Mark Howe.

"Hope in Jesus', "The greatest need" and "Quality of life" have been translated and adapted from messages written in French by David Buick.

"A change of heart" was written by Mark Howe.

"Famous last words" was originally written by John Robertson. The message was recorded by David Fanstone, and has been modified for inclusion in this handbook.

In the interest of brevity the messages have been recorded in a highly abbreviated form, and will need to be expanded by the preacher. Two diagrams are shown for each message: the left-hand one shows the state of the sketchboard at the beginning of the message, while the right-hand one shows the finished painting. Words that are to be written on the sketchboard are shown in the text as block capitals, and other additions to the painting are shown in the margins. Asterisks show the point at which these additions should be painted up.

What do you follow?

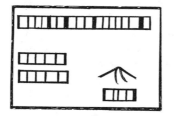 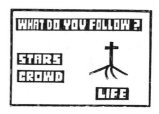

Attention

I'd like to ask you a question ... WHAT DO YOU FOLLOW? Each of us has hobbies and interests and things which we follow.

Interest

Some people follow STARS, the horoscopes. They get up in the morning, open the paper, it says, "You'll have a great day, meet someone really good-looking and fall in love". The problem with following the stars is that often we let our whole lives revolve around what the papers say.

Spiritual concern

Following the stars will never meet the need in your life. That need is not something we can change, because it is caused by the position we are in. The wrong things we do and say have separated us* from a life of meaning and joy, and from the one who made us, and who made the stars.

I used to follow the CROWD. I realised that something was missing in my life and thought that other people had the answer. I followed the crowd for many years: I tried wine, women, sex and drugs, but following the crowd never got rid of that minus sign in my life. Instead of bringing satisfaction and peace it left me even more dissatisfied.

Application

Following the crowd will never give you what you are looking for, but I follow someone who has promised me life, and life to the full. That person is God.

We are separated from God because of the things which we have done wrong in our lives – the Bible tells us that God can't look at us because of our

127

sin. But because God loved us so much, he sent his son Jesus 2000 years ago.* He died on a cross to pay the penalty for all our sins. He's alive today and he can make your life something wonderful.

Response

For 2000 years many millions have followed Jesus and found the answer to LIFE. Jesus offers you that same chance now. You have to admit that you need forgiveness, believe that Jesus died in your place and commit your life to following him day by day. Will anyone choose to follow Jesus today?

Miami Vice[1]

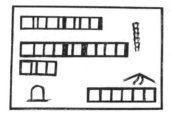

Attention

Good afternoon. I would like to talk about one of my favourite TV programmes: MIAMI VICE.

Interest

This show has everything: beautiful men and women, homes, cars and palm trees.* I'm not very

1. This message is included to show how a topical subject, such as a TV programme, can form the basis of a Gospel presentation.

good at drawing all these things but I'm super at drawing palm trees. This afternoon I want to suggest to you that vice is not limited to Miami: there is as much vice right here.

Spiritual concern

Vice is something that we all participate in. In Italy they recognised this, and one of their most popular shows asked this question; WHAT'S YOUR VICE? They went all over the country and found people who committed the 7 deadly sins. This afternoon I want to ask you the same question. What's your vice? (Leave a pregnant pause. Talk about the sin that was in your life before you were saved.)

We all have a problem, in that our lives are constantly being ruined by the wrong things we do and say. Worse still, vice eventually leads here* the graveyard (talk about how drugs etc. can kill). The wrong things we do also lead to spiritual death.

God doesn't want that. He wants us to be alive, to know him and walk with him.

Application

Some people try to find God on their own. However this is impossible: you don't see corpses bringing themselves back to life. When you're dead you're dead. That's why Jesus came.* He died for our sin and vice. When he rose from the dead he made it possible for us to receive him into our lives and to become alive to God by knowing him personally (talk about how you discovered a new life in Jesus).

Response

You can have this new life today. You need to ACCEPT your need of forgiveness and be prepared to turn from your sin, putting Jesus in charge of your life.

True love

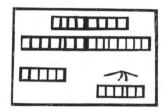 

Attention

Today I am going to talk about something that all of you would like to have today: LOVE. But that word doesn't mean much nowadays. The sort of love that we want is . . .

Interest

. . . TRUE LOVE. And I'm sure that you've seen the films. The hero is walking down a street, all alone. Suddenly he sees her. She sees him Their eyes meet, and you know it must be true love. But very often it doesn't last, because the characters in the film turn out to be SELFISH. The man only wants the woman for her body, the woman only wants the man for his money, and what we thought was true love turns out to be simple selfishness.

Spiritual concern

The reason that there are so many films like that is because there are so many lives like that. You have probably been hurt by other people's selfishness. My trouble is that I find the people who hurt me are rather like ... me! None of us is perfect, and because of our selfishness the chances are that many of us will end up ...

Application

... ALONE. Marriages and families break up because the partners want to take, not give. And you can be alone, even with lots of friends or a big family. The good news is that there is someone who really loves you. That person is God. Now I'm not going to talk about religion today. Actually you can go to church, pray, confess your sins, but none of those things will deal with the real problem; your sinfulness.

And that's why Jesus came to earth 2000 years ago.* He lived a perfect life for 30 years. And then he showed us God's love by dying on a cross. He took the punishment that you and I deserve.

Response

Three days later he rose again. He is alive today and you can meet him, if only you are willing to DECIDE. True love is not about a funny feeling in your stomach. To find the true love of God you have to decide to put him first for the rest of your life and to accept his free gift of eternal life. I did that a number of years ago, and although my life hasn't been perfect since, I can tell you that God has been FAITHFUL. Who would like to find true love today?

What do You want?

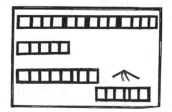

Attention

Good afternoon! I have an important issue to talk to you about . . . WHAT DO YOU WANT?

Interest

Some want financial security, so they make this the centre of their lives: MONEY (describe working patterns). They think that if they can only make enough money they will be safe.

The problem is that financial security can be gone in a matter of seconds: (Wall Street Crash).

I want to tell you about someone who has control over the world's financial institutions, governments and corporations. Yet this same person gave away all he had so that he would be able to identify with you and me.

Our quest for money separates us from him and we have become poor because of it.

Spiritual concern

I used to want a personal relationship with God. I felt alone and I wanted to know the one in charge. So I tried this: MORALITY. A lot of people are trying this today. They think that going to church is all they need. But you can sit in church or be out doing good and still be a million miles from God.

Jesus is not about religion.* He is about goodness, love, joy, peace and justice. When people meet him they meet God.

Application

Jesus came to show us God, and when he died he was dying for the rotten things in you and I which separate us from God. You see God is holy and clean while we're sinful and dirty. Jesus died for our sins. And when he rose from the dead he made it possible for us to meet God. If we make him the boss of our lives we can be forgiven and know God personally. (Testimony).

Response

You can know God today through one person: CHRIST. (Invitation.)

Something beautiful

Attention

I'm not a mind-reader, but I'm sure that this is something that you'd like to be . . .

Interest

. . . SOMETHING BEAUTIFUL. Today we spend millions of pounds on looking our best. When you get up in the morning you have a wash, comb your hair, have a shave (if you're a man) and then choose your best clothes. And I can see that you have succeeded.

Spiritual concern

Actually I would know that even if I couldn't see you. The world's best-selling book tells us that we are all wonderfully made. But although you look great on the outside, on the inside you may be . . .

Application

. . . BROKEN. Perhaps because of something someone once said, perhaps because you have been let down. And probably you have hurt other people too. That best-selling book, the Bible, also tells us that all of us fall short of what we ought to be. Because of our selfishness society is divided,* and individuals are . . .

. . . EMPTY. You may feel that life is not worth living, that something is missing in your life. Blaise Pascal said that we all have a God-shaped hole in our lives. Jesus came to fill that emptiness.*

Jesus knows all about you. And yet he loved you enough to die on a cross, and even to go to hell so that you don't have to. Three days later he rose again and now you can meet him. But you need to be willing to . . .

Response

. . . CHANGE. Are you willing to let God take away the things that you know are wrong in your life? Are you willing to believe that you can only be forgiven because of the death of Jesus? Are you willing to follow him for the rest of your life? When you turn to God in this way you start to become SOMETHING BEAUTIFUL FOR GOD. (Invitation.)

Happiness

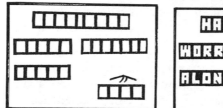 

Attention

I want to talk today about something that all of us are looking for . . . HAPPINESS.

Interest

Some people look for job satisfaction, others look for enough earnings to buy their happiness. Maybe you look for love and acceptance in your family, or maybe you watch the television to forget about all your problems. But for many people their happiness is spoilt by . . .

Spiritual concern

. . . WORRY. We worry about losing our jobs or friends. We worry that if our friends really knew what we're like they wouldn't like us any more. Other people worry about things that happened in the past: "If only I could take back those things I said!" Perhaps your biggest worry is this . . .

Application

... being ALONE. On the outside everything looks great, but inside we never relax in case people see the "real me". Then there will be no-one who cares for us. A few years ago I felt that I had no real friends at all. Then a somebody told me some good news: there was someone who knew all the things that I'd done and yet still loved me. He knows all about you too. That person is God. But you are separated from him by your selfishness. God wants to be your closest friend, and so to deal with that barrier of your sin he sent Jesus.* (Explain the cross and the resurrection.) But to meet him you need to TURN to him.

Response

I realised that my life was a mess. I admitted to myself and to God that I had done lots of wrong things. I believed that Jesus the Son of God died for my sins and rose again. I asked God to be the most important person in my life.

Sometimes I still have problems, but I know that the happiness and the life that God gives will last FOREVER. (Invitation.)

The whole truth

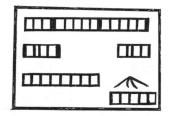 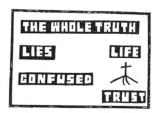

Attention

I wonder if you could move in a bit so that I don't get into trouble with the police. Otherwise I could find myself in court being asked for this . . .

Interest

. . . THE WHOLE TRUTH. Our legal system relies on the honesty of witnesses. And many people today are searching for truth in their lives. Something to hold on to; something that can be trusted. But instead we often find . . .

Spiritual concern

. . . LIES. Your boyfriend swears he loves you, then the next day he's off with your best friend. Your boss says you're his best employee, then suddenly you find yourself on the dole. And of course all of us lie from time to time. How many times have you staggered into work in the morning after a terrible night, and when someone asks how you are, you say "Fine!" Often we lie to cover up the

138

things that we know are wrong in our lives. Because of all these lies we end up . . .

Application

. . . CONFUSED. Who can you trust? All the politicians claim to have the answers, all the religions claim to know the truth. But today you can meet someone who said "I *am* the Truth." That person is Jesus.* When he spoke people knew what he said was right. And for speaking the truth his enemies took him, beat him and nailed him to a cross. Jesus had never been separated from his Father in heaven, but on the cross God turned his back on him because of your lies and my lies. He died in our place.

Jesus rose from the dead and you can meet him by deciding to . . .

Response

. . . TRUST. Look at the life of Jesus, and you will see that he is worth trusting. Stop trying to find God on your own: admit that you deserve nothing but rejection from God, but that because of Jesus' death you can be accepted. Follow him day by day. Jesus also tells us that he is the LIFE: He can give you a life that starts now and will go on forever. (Invitation.)

Hope in Jesus

Attention

I would like to talk to you about something that we all need to have to make life worth living: HOPE

Interest

I would like to write up three words on my sketchboard, things that people hope for. First of all there is PEACE (give examples). Secondly, there is TRUTH (more examples). My number three, which is perhaps the world's number one wish, is LOVE. Psychologists tell us that our most pressing need is to have someone to love, and even more so someone to love us.

Spiritual concern

That's what we hope for, but what's life really like? When we hope for peace, we often find STRESS. We long for truth, but we often find nothing but LIES, in all areas of our lives. And how about love? Today there are lots of broken hearts about, full of HATE. And one day along comes something to put an end to our hoping once and for all: DEATH. It is tragic that you can spend your whole life trying to satisfy your hopes. It is as if there is a barrier which stops us ever getting them. Why?*

Application

Actually, all these bad things come out of our heart. It is part of our human nature that we are not perfect, and so we can never live up to our ideals. But you know there is someone who is perfect, who wants to give us LIFE and who has smashed through this barrier: JESUS. On the cross he paid the price for all the bad things that are in your heart and mine, and he offers us the chance to find lasting peace, real truth and true love through a living personal relationship with God.

Response

What do you need to do? Just one thing . . . HOPE IN JESUS (explain and give invitation.)

The greatest need

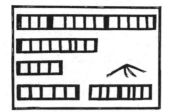 

Attention

I would like to ask you a question today: what do you think is THE GREATEST NEED in your life?

Interest

We all look for SECURITY. Sometimes we need HELP. And everyone wants their life to make SENSE. Where do we look for these things? Many look for security in money, but money doesn't offer happiness or security. When we need help, we look to our friends, but even our closest friends let us down from time to time, and a lot of people have no real friends at all. We look just about everywhere to find meaning in life. Some people rely on astrologers to guide them, but no two horoscopes say the same thing: how can they be trusted?

Spiritual concern

There are lots of people who say that there is no God because they have never received any of these things from him. But the problem is not with God . . .

Application

God exists all right, and he wants to give us all these things and more besides, but we have turned him down. Every single one of us has decided to run his own life, without wanting to pay attention to what God says. And because of this there is a barrier between us and him,* we have rebelled against him. Now we try all kinds of ways to get through this barrier, by religion, by leading a good life,* but the problem of rebellion in our heart is not solved. God had to break through this barrier himself* (explain the life, death and resurrection of Jesus).

Response

God offers us everything we need, if only we are ready to admit that we need him (explain repentance). He offers us our greatest need of all: NEW LIFE (explain forgiveness and being born again and give invitation.)

A change of heart

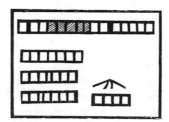 

Attention

As you trudge from shop to shop today, it is quite likely that you are looking for this ... A CHANGE

Interest

Maybe you are unhappy about your job, your family or your neighbours. It is very interesting to note that a few years ago people would naturally go to the vicar with problems like this. Nowadays people look to doctors, or even to psychologists. So what do psychologists say about change?

Some say that we need to change our PARENTS. Apparently all our problems start because of the way we are brought up, or even because of things that we inherit from our parents.

Spiritual concern

Now the snag is as follows: if I have a problem because my parents have problems, presumably they have problems because of their parents, and so on. On that basis we are all in the same boat.

144

It's as if the whole human race is suffering from the same disease, a selfishness which leads to everything from fights in the playground to world war. In fact the best-selling book in the world states that throughout the whole of history only one man has not been affected by this disease.

Other psychologists tell us that we need to change SOCIETY. If we can change a man's environment we can change his lifestyle. There are lots of ideas about what is wrong with the world and how to put it right. But as someone once said, "The difference between capitalism and communism is that in capitalism man exploits man and in communism it's the other way round"! None of the political systems ever invented can solve the world's problems, because, as the Good Book says, the problems come from our hearts.

Application

Now as my mother was always telling me when I was younger, this group of people can also change us for better or worse: FRIENDS. Have you ever noticed that when you are out with your friends you are willing to do all sorts of things which you would never do on your own, and which you regret afterwards? We all need friends who will stand by us, no matter what, friends who will LOVE us for what we are. Yet so often we blow it. I have a friend who has promised never to leave me or forsake me. That person is God.

You see God loves you and wants to be your friend. But first of all he had to do something about your selfishness. God is perfect and when he sees the way we treat each other and ignore him he feels ANGER. The love and anger of God come together in this person.

*Jesus is the only man who never deserved to be punished. Yet God poured all his anger at mankind into Jesus' body while he was hanging on the cross. Jesus died in our place. Three days later he rose again, to prove that he had conquered death once and for all.

Response

You can be changed from the inside out by meeting Jesus. But you need to be ready, not just for a change of attitude, but for A CHANGE OF HEART. Are you ready for God to make you the person you were always intended to be?

Famous last words

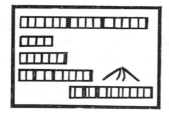
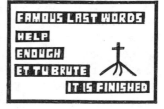

Attention

It seems that many people are interested in quiz shows, quiz games or quiz books. I am going to write up the title for my own street quiz . . . FAMOUS LAST WORDS.

Interest

The last words of a person can tell us a lot about that person's priorities during life and attitude towards death. Now can anyone tell me the last words of . . . John Lennon? Yes, HELP. Here was a man who had everything: money, success, a loving family. Yet when he was shot outside his New York apartment, none of those things could help him.

Spiritual concern

You may be completely satisfied with your lifestyle today, but will your satisfaction last? As the old proverb says, there is a way that seems right to a man, but in the end it leads to death.

Now a more difficult question. What were the last words . . . Emmanuel Shinwell? No? He said "I've had ENOUGH". After one hundred years of life and a long career as a member of parliament he had had enough.

Application

Now you all look young and healthy, but judging from the suicide statistics there are many young people who are fed up with life too. I have a friend who gives me a life with meaning and purpose. Not everyone has such good friends. Does anyone know the last words of Julius Caesar according to Shakespeare? That's right, ET TU BRUTE. Julius Caesar was betrayed by his best friend. You may feel that you don't have a friend in the world, but as the Bible says, there is a friend who sticks closer than a brother.

God can be your closest friend because he knows you better than anyone else. He knows that the wrong things in your life will eventually destroy you if they are not dealt with. That's why he was willing to come to earth, to die on a cross.* On that cross he was punished for your sin and mine. That means that you don't have to live with the consequences of your past any more.

Response

The last words of Jesus on the cross were IT IS FINISHED. He has done all that is necessary to give you a new life that lasts for ever. Are you prepared to give the rest of your life to him? (Invitation.)

Quality of life

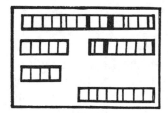 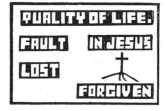

Attention

Hello! I'd like to talk to you about something we're all looking for ... QUALITY. We want quality homes, quality food, quality holidays... in fact QUALITY OF LIFE. Quality is becoming more and more important to us.

Interest

And why not? We're pretty top quality ourselves aren't we? The Bible tells us we are wonderfully made. But what about quality control? You know what often happens when you buy some high-quality merchandise: you get it back home, and suddenly, there's a FAULT – usually discovered two days after the guarantee runs out! So you have to go back and complain, and it's all very annoying.

Spiritual concern

We're like that too: although we are wonderfully made, there are things in our lives that mean we're not perfect; things we do and think that make other people reject us and make us hate ourselves on the inside, because we know they're wrong. What happens to the faulty product? It gets thrown away. That's bad news for the manufacturer, because it's LOST: no use at all. And it's just the same with us. Because of the things that are wrong in our lives, we're lost in the eyes of our creator The Bible says that the wrong things in our lives separate us from God. We try to improve the quality of our lives in many ways, but we can never succeed while we're cut off from the one who made us.

Application

But God loves us and doesn't want to leave us on the scrapheap. He loves us so much that even though we were lost in his eyes, he crossed the barrier between us and him by sending his Son Jesus.* And Jesus showed people what real quality was all about. He lived a perfect life. People weren't attracted to him by his money or his social circle, but by his life, lived in total harmony with God, and by his love for them. When Jesus died on the cross, it was no accident: it was to pay the price for all the faults in our lives, all the things that separate us from God. Jesus rose from the dead three days later to prove his victory over evil and to show us that the way back to God had been opened.

Response

How can we find the way back to God? We have to do something that's both simple and difficult; we have to be FORGIVEN for the wrong things we've done, for leaving God out of our life, and ask him to come into our life to make it what he wants it to be. We have to be ready for God to change our lives. If we are willing to do this, God promises us true quality of life IN JESUS. Jesus tells us that he came into the world so that we can have abundant life. He showed us that this didn't mean a life without hardship or suffering – but a living relationship with God who loves us. It's the most fantastic kind of life there is! (Possible testimony.) Who would like to receive this abundant life from Jesus today?

31: Sketchboard messages for children

"Seventy times seven" was written by Pauline Nix.
"Samson" was written by Susan Howe.
"Barabbas" has appeared in many forms. This version is by Mark Detzler, based on another version by Paul Morley.
"The call of Moses" was written by Mark Howe.
"The feeding of the five thousand", "the paralytic" and "the good shepherd" were written by Dawn Clancy.
"Bartimaeus" and "Naaman" are OAC favourites. These versions were provided by Dawn Clancy.
"Creation" was written by Susan Howe.

Seventy times seven

Introduction

Do you like maths? Before I tell you the story here is a little maths test. Who knows 7×7?* What about 7×10?* This is a hard one: 70×7 (children usually get this wrong; 70, 77, 140 etc., leave answer blank).

7×7= 49

7 × 10 = 70
70 × 7 =

Peter, one of Jesus friends, couldn't do this sum either. Peter asked Jesus how many times should he forgive someone, as many as 7 times? Jesus said "No, 70 × 7 times", and while Peter was working out the answer Jesus told this story.

Story

There was once a rich man settling his accounts. He found that one of his servants owed him £1000?* So he called him in to explain the debt (check children understand debt). The servant couldn't pay and knew it: the punishment for not paying was prison.

We are all like that servant. Our debt is to God. The problem is not money, but the wrong things we do (give examples). We can't pay the debt. One day we'll stand before God and he'll ask us to explain or take the punishment.

The servant got on his knees and asked the rich man to be patient. The rich man saw how sorry he was and decided to forgive him. He took his red pen and crossed out the servant's account.*

God loves us and has provided a way to cancel our account too. He wants to forgive the wrong things we've done. He sent Jesus, who never did anything wrong, to die on a cross in our place.* If we ask Jesus to forgive us he places his cross over our account, so when God looks at us he doesn't see a list of wrong things, but the cross of Jesus cancelling it out.

This is not the end of the story. The servant went on his way*and met a friend who owed him £5.* Instead of forgiving him as he'd been forgiven, he grabbed him round the throat and demanded his £5 back. The friend couldn't pay so the servant had him thrown into prison. The rich man got to hear about this and was angry with his servant. He called him back: "I forgave you but you didn't forgive others, so because you haven't acted to others as I did to you, you'll be thrown into prison."

70 × 7 = 490. If we ask Jesus to forgive us we need to forgive others when they do unkind or wrong things to us too. (Invitation.)*

Samson

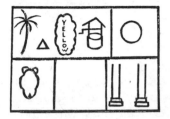 

1: The birth of Samson

One day a woman was at a well,* collecting water, when she saw a bright light. In the light there was an angel.* The woman was very frightened, but the angel spoke to her. He said, "You are going to have a son who will be very special. He will start to free your people from the Philistines. You must not cut his hair, as a sign that he is special to God."

Sure enough the woman did give birth to a big, strong, bouncing baby. His parents called him Samson.

2: Samson and the lion

As Samson grew up he soon realised that he was bigger and stronger than all his friends. One day he was walking along thinking about what he would have for tea when he heard a loud roar. It was a lion.* Samson turned round, and before he knew what had happened he had killed the lion with his bare hands.

God had started to give Samson the strength he needed to get rid of the Philistines. God says that each one of us is special. There are things that he wants you to do for him. Whenever God asks us to do something he gives us the strength we need to do it.

3: Samson and Delilah

Samson started to chase the Philistines out of his country. But he began to forget about God and to rely on his own strength. One day he saw the most beautiful girl he had ever seen.* Her name was Delilah, and Samson fell madly in love with her.

Now Delilah was a Philistine, and the Philistine leaders told her that if she found the secret of Samson's strength they would give her lots of money. So Delilah asked Samson what made him so strong. Samson said that if someone tied him up with new bowstrings he would lose his strength. Delilah tried this, but it didn't work. Then Samson said that someone would have to tie him up with new ropes, but that didn't work either. Delilah kept asking Samson for the secret, and Samson kept making up different answers.

You might have thought that Samson would realise that something was going on. Maybe this was God's way of trying to warn him. Often when we disobey God he warns us through other people or the Bible.

4: Samson loses his strength

Eventually Samson gave in and told Delilah that if someone cut his hair he would lose his strength. Delilah waited until Samson was asleep and then cut off all his hair.* The Philistines came and took him away. They laughed at him and made Samson work for them. If we ignore what God says to us things will go wrong.

5: The death of Samson

The Philistines organised a big party, and decided to chain Samson up in the middle of the hall so that everyone could laugh at him.* Samson realised how silly he had been. He prayed to God and asked for one more chance to obey him. Then he realised that his hair had started to grow back. Samson pushed as hard as he could against the pillars and the roof of the hall collapsed.*Samson was killed, but so were hundreds of the Philistine leaders who had been so cruel to his people.

If we pray to God, telling him how sorry we are for disobeying him, God will forgive us and will be able to use us again. God can forgive us because of what Jesus has done. Samson did lots of things wrong before he died. Jesus never did anything bad at all, but he was killed for all the wrong things that all of us have done. When we ask Jesus to be our friend he will help us to do what God wants.

Barabbas

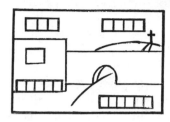 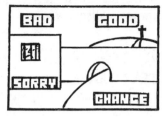

Attention and interest

Who do you think this is?*He's a man, a man who is unhappy. Why is he unhappy?* He's in prison. The walls are streaming with water. There are big fat rats that eat his porridge, and when there's no porridge left they nibble his toes. Why do you think he's in prison?

Spiritual concern

Because he was BAD. It started when he was young, disobeying his mum. One thing led to another. We are like this: telling lies to cover up wrong actions. He had his own gang, and he did lots of bad things until one day the soldiers caught him and took him to Pontius Pilate, the judge. He sentenced Barabbas to death. So here he is in prison waiting to die.

Another man was around at the same time and he was GOOD. Who do you think that was? When Jesus did good things most people were very happy but some were angry and jealous. One day they got him into trouble and brought him before Pontius Pilate. Barabbas can hear the crowds because the

158

trial is outside. Pilate was big and fat but he had a very high voice – he says, "Who should I release to you, Jesus or Barabbas?" Barabbas cannot hear him, he can only hear the crowd. The crowd shouts, "Barabbas!" Pilate says, "What should I do with Jesus then?" The crowd shouts, "Crucify him!" All Barabbas hears is his name and "Crucify him!"

Application

Suddenly he feels SORRY (list all the things he's sorry for). While this is happening Jesus is being crucified.* (Explain the atonement.) Three days later he rose from the dead so that he could be our friend. A guard comes along while Barabbas is in prison. Barabbas does not understand what has happened and thinks the guard has come to take him away – he's very frightened (act all this out). The guard says to Barabbas, "You don't have to die today, Jesus has died for you". He is set free.

Response

Barabbas went out of the city and saw the cross of Jesus. We don't know what he did next, but since then thousands and millions have thought about the cross of Jesus. They have become sorry that they were bad and wanted to be good. So they have asked Jesus to help them to CHANGE. (Finish with personal testimony.)

The call of Moses

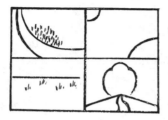

Our story starts in Egypt.* A woman is walking by a river. There are crowds of attendants around her. They are looking into the rushes and they see ... a basket.* The basket is coated with tar. And inside there is a baby. Who hid the baby? The mother, because the Egyptians were killing all the baby boys. The woman told one of the servants to fetch the baby. She was the Pharaoh's daughter. She took the baby to the palace and adopted him. The baby was called Moses.

God protected Moses because he had a purpose for his life. Moses was going to save his people from the Egyptians. God has a purpose for each of you too. But we need to wait for God to show us what he wants us to do.

As Moses grew up he couldn't wait for God. One day he was out walking when he saw an Egyptian beating up one of his people. He was so angry he killed the Egyptian and hid his body.* He thought no-one had seen him. But a bit later he discovered that people had found out.

Perhaps when you do wrong things you try to

hide them. But very often people find out. And even if no-one else sees, God knows about everything that we do. When we disobey God things go wrong.

Moses was frightened that he would get into trouble for killing a man. So he ran away and went to live in the desert. He found a job as a shepherd, he married a young girl and little by little he forgot about all his ideas of saving his people. After all, he had disobeyed God: how could God use him now? Then one day he saw a burning bush.* As he approached a voice came out of the bush: it was God speaking to him! Moses took off his shoes and listened to God's plan for his life.*

God can forgive us for all the naughty things that we do. He can forgive us because of what Jesus has done for us* (explain cross). And as well as forgiving us he can use us to help other people and to tell them about him (testimony).

Feeding the five thousand

Attention and interest

It was the middle of the half-term holiday and Tom was bored. There was nothing left to do or to play. "Why don't you go fishing", said mum, "I'll make

you a packed lunch and you can stay all day".
"Wow, brilliant", said Tom, and went to get all
his gear together.

Tom set off down to the lake and was soon
happily fishing in his favourite spot, when he
watched a boat pull up and out got thirteen men.*
One of them seemed to be the leader, and he soon
sat down and began to talk to all the others. Tom
began to half-listen to what he was saying. This
man was a brilliant storyteller. As he listened, he
noticed there were more and more people coming
to join the group.* He didn't know where they
were all coming from, but there seemed to be thousands of them, all sitting down on the grass listening to what the man said. Does anyone know who
it was? That's right, it was Jesus. He looked round
at all the people and knew that they all had the
same problem, "I" disease, that was making a mess
of their lives.

Spiritual concern and application

We all know what that is don't we? 'I want this, I
want that, I want what I want and I want it now."
Those people were no different to us were they?
Well they listened to Jesus for a very long time.
All the way through lunch time and all the way
through tea time without noticing it. Can you
imagine that, fancy listening to one of your
teachers all day and not realising you hadn't eaten!
As it began to get dark, Jesus said to his disciples,
"These people are hungry, give them something to
eat!" The disciples looked at each other. They
hadn't got any food, and it would cost pounds and

pounds to feed all these people: what could they do?

Tom suddenly remembered his picnic lunch. He could give that to them, but that would be too small. Jesus wouldn't want to be bothered with that. We sometimes feel like that don't we? That we don't have very much to offer and Jesus wouldn't be able to use us, but Tom was about to find out just what Jesus could do with something very small. He went up to Andrew. "Please sir, I've got some food, you can use that." The other disciples told Andrew not to be so silly, but he took Tom to Jesus. "This little boy has some food: five loaves and two small fish." Jesus took the food, and thanked God for it, then they made all the people sit down and Jesus began to break up the food and gave it to the disciples to take round. They kept on coming back for more, and more, and more; and it didn't run out until every one of the people had eaten enough. Not only that, but Jesus sent the disciples round collecting up all the leftovers, and there were twelve baskets full of them! Incredible! When one young boy gives what he has to Jesus, Jesus PROVIDES enough food for the entire crowd.

But you know Jesus knew that the people had a much bigger need than being fed. Do you know what it was? That's right, they needed to have their "I" disease cured, and Jesus was going on to do something about that too. Later on he died on the cross.* When he died on the cross he was being punished. Now we get punished when we do something wrong, don't we? Did Jesus ever do anything wrong? No. But I just said he was being punished!

163

He was being punished for all the wrong things that people like Tom had done, that I've done and that everyone who believes and trusts in him has done.

Response

When I was younger I told Jesus I was very sorry for all the wrong things in my life and asked him to forgive me. I didn't have a packed lunch to give to him, but I gave him myself, and that's why I'm standing here today telling you this story, because that's the way Jesus wants to use me. I wonder how he wants to use you if you give yourself to him?

The Paralytic

Attention and interest

Can you wriggle your fingers? Toes? Shoulders? Can you sit absolutely still, and not move a muscle? Isn't it horrible not being able to move? I want to tell you about a boy called Tim who couldn't move at all, not ever, he was paralysed. He couldn't run around and play football or go skateboarding, all he could do was lie there on his mat all day. Do you think he had a really exciting life? No! One day Tim's four friends were reading the newspaper when they saw that JESUS was coming to town. "Hey Jesus makes people better, I'm sure he could do something for Tim, let's take him to Jesus". So they rushed round to Tim's house and knocked at the door. Tim got up to answer it . . . Oh no he didn't did he? "Tim, Jesus is coming to town and we think he could make you better, we'll take you to him". "Oh, Jesus won't want to be bothered with me, he'll be far too busy with all the important people."

Spiritual concern and application

We sometimes feel like that, don't we? But you know Jesus is interested in all of us, no matter how unimportant we may feel. The four friends picked up Tim's mat and carried him to the house where Jesus was, but when they got there, it was surrounded by loads and loads of people.* "We'll never get in there". "Oh yes we will, let's try the window". But there were people all around that too. "I know, the roof, come on!" They went up the steps onto the roof* and the four friends began to dig through it.* The folk inside wondered what was happening as bits of roof began to fall on their heads. Tim's friends made a hole right over where Jesus was standing and lowered Tim carefully through the hole until he was right in front of Jesus.*

Jesus looked down at Tim, and Tim looked up at Jesus and he could see just one thing in Jesus' face . . . LOVE. "But he shouldn't love me"

thought Tim, "I've thought and said so many bad things". He wanted to hide away because he felt as if Jesus could see right through him and see all the bad things, but Jesus said something amazing. He looked at Tim and said "I FORGIVE you". Tim was amazed, all the people were very angry. "How can he forgive sin, only God can do that, how dare he". They didn't know that Jesus really was God, and that later on he was going to do something very special so that he could forgive the sin of everyone who believes and trusts in him.

Jesus knew exactly what they were all thinking, so he said, "Which is easier, to say your sin is forgiven or to say 'stand up and walk'?" All the people went quiet. Jesus looked at Tim and said, "Stand up, pick up your bed and walk!" Tim felt a tingling all over him. He moved his feet, his hands, his legs. He got up and picked up his bed and began to dance round the room. "I can move, I can walk, I can run"! He sang and danced all the way home.

Response

You know I was just as excited as that when I found out that Jesus LOVES me and that he FOR-GIVES me for all the wrong things in my life. You see I said to Jesus, "I'm really sorry for all the wrong things I've done, please will you forgive me and make me clean inside?" Jesus could do that for me because he died on the cross.* When he did that he was being punished for all the wrong things I have done, and for everyone who believes and trusts in him. But he didn't stay dead did he? And because he is alive today he can love us and forgive us now. Knowing Jesus loves and forgives you is just as fantastic as Tim being able to walk again!

The good shepherd

Attention

Today I would like to tell you a story about some-one you might recognise. I'll paint him up on my sketchboard.* Can you see who it is? Yes, it's a sheep! We'll call him Baaaarnaby. Can you say that? Barnaby and his friends were cared for by someone very special. What do we call a person whose job it is to look after sheep? That's right a SHEPHERD. There is someone who wants to look after us and keep us safe too.

Interest

One night the shepherd was counting his sheep into the sheepfold for the night: seventy-six, sev-enty-seven; ninety-five, ninety-six, ninety-seven, ninety-eight, ninety-nine . . . oh no! There should be 100! The shepherd was going to count his flock again, but the ninety-nine sheep soon told him who was missing: Baaaarnaby!

Earlier that day, Barnaby had looked around the field of green grass, and said to himself. "I'm bored. I don't want to eat green grass. I want to eat red flowers." And there was a clump of delicious red flowers just a little way away. So off he went. Then he saw some more red flowers . . . and soon he was heading up a mountainside, far away from the rest of the flock. Suddenly, just as he reached for a particularly yummy flower, his foot slipped, and became caught between two rocks. Well, he could still reach the red flowers, but soon he realised that he was . . . TRAPPED.

Spiritual concern

Barnaby was in real trouble. Soon it would be dark. And often we get ourselves trapped don't we? Maybe we tell one little white lie. And then we have to tell another lie to cover up the first one. And soon we have told so many lies that we can hardly remember what the truth is. Fortunately, the shepherd worked out where Barnaby had gone, and came looking for him. Barnaby called out to the shepherd, and soon he was rescued. Maybe you call out to God when you're in trouble too.

Barnaby had been so frightened by his adventure that he was good for a whole two days. But then he became bored. "I want to eat red flowers", he thought.* Off he went again, and soon he found himself in a big black wood. In the wood, there was a big, black bear, who was very hungry. Just as the bear was going to have Barnaby for lunch, the shepherd arrived. You see, Barnaby didn't realise that he was IN DANGER. And sometimes we put ourselves in danger. Perhaps we play where we shouldn't, or talk to strangers that we shouldn't.

Barnaby saw the big, black bear as it ran back into the big, black forest, and he was so frightened that he was good for a two whole weeks. But then he was bored again. This time he sneaked past the sheepdogs, and soon he was munching the red flowers. Soon there was only one left, and as he stretched out to eat it, he fell over a ledge.* As he lay there, out of sight, he realised that he was LOST. Barnaby thought he had run off once too often, that the shepherd wouldn't look for him this time. And some people think that they have done too many wrong things to ever be accepted by God.

Application

But the shepherd set off with his dogs and his lantern, to look for Barnaby. Barnaby was calling out to the shepherd in desperation, and when the shepherd heard him, he looked over the side and saw his lost sheep. The shepherd climbed down the side of the ledge to rescue Barnaby. He got scratched and bruised and cut by the rocks and the brambles, but he didn't mind, as long as he could save his lost sheep. Jesus came to rescue us from all the wrong things that we have done. He even died, to save me and all his other lost sheep.*

Response

The shepherd picked up Barnaby in his arms and carried him to safety. The lost sheep had been SAVED. When I called out to Jesus, and told him how sorry I was for all the selfish things I had done wrong, he saved me. He wants to save each one of us, because he loves us. The Bible says that Jesus is THE GOOD SHEPHERD. We can call out to him at any time, because he is always listening.

Bartimaeus

Attention and interest

I want you to use your imagination. Over here we have a house. Inside the house is a young lady, outside the house is her husband and he's in a terrible state: (pacing) "Oh dear, oh dear, what shall I do? Read a book? Have a cup of tea! No, oh dear, oh dear." What's going on inside? Yes, his wife is having a baby. He was a beautiful baby, and his dad decided to call him this: BARTI-MAEUS. As he grew up his mum and dad noticed that he kept on bumping into things and they realised that he was BLIND. Now that was terrible! Nowadays if someone is blind we know how to help them to lead a normal life, but in those days there was nothing. Do you think he would have a nice life? No!

Spiritual concern

You know each one of us has something which stops us from having all the best things in life . . . "I" disease. You know, "I want this, I want that, I want what I want and I want it now!" Well, because he couldn't go out to work, Bartimaeus had to go with his father down to the market and there they bought a special cloak for him. It was like a badge telling everyone that Bartimaeus was a BEGGAR, and that's just how people with "I" disease end up, begging to be told how to get the best out of life, how to have a good life. Every day Bartimaeus would go down to the gate of the city and sit begging.

One day he heard a great crowd coming. "What's happening?" Oh be quiet you silly old beggar!" Do you think he would be quiet? No! "What's going on?" "Jesus is coming to town, now be quiet." Jesus . . . Jesus . . . didn't he make a dead girl live the other day? Hey, he could make me see! So Bartimaeus listened until he was sure Jesus was close by . . . "Jesus, son of David, have mercy on me!" The people all told him to shut up, but do you think he would? No, he shouted again, and this time Jesus heard him and told his disciples to bring Bartimaeus to him. As he got up he did an amazing thing: he threw off his beggar's cloak: he was never going back to begging.

171

Application

Jesus asked Bartimaeus a really strange question: "WHAT DO YOU WANT?" Well, do you think Bartimaeus said: "Jesus I'm really hungry, could you buy me some fish and chips?" Or how about "Jesus I'm very poor, could you give me a thousand pounds?" No! He said, "Jesus it's my eyes. I want to see!" Jesus looked at him and he could see just what he was like on the inside. He could see that Bartimaeus BELIEVED, so he said to him, "Your faith has healed you." Bartimaeus looked down . . . hands . . . feet . . . people . . . I can see! I can see! Look everybody, I can see! Jesus has made me see!" You've never seen anyone as excited as Bartimaeus was.*

Response

One day I got just as excited as Bartimaeus because I found out that Jesus could take away my "I" disease as well. To do that he had to do something very special. He died on the cross.* When he died on the cross he was being punished. Now we get punished when we do wrong things don't we? Did Jesus ever do anything wrong? But I just said he was being punished. He was being punished for all the wrong things people like Bartimaeus do, all the wrong things I do and all the wrong things that everyone who believes and trusts in him has done. When I was younger I said to Jesus, "I'm really sorry for all the wrong things I've done, please will you forgive me and get rid of all my "I" disease and help me to follow you." Do you know, he did that, and I've been following Jesus ever since, and it's the best life ever, following Jesus.

Naaman

Attention and interest

I want to tell you about someone who was very famous, one of these . . . A GENERAL. He was a very good general, and was so famous that every morning he had to do chest-expanding exercises so that his chest was big enough to pin all his medals on. One Saturday night it was bath night as usual, and things were fine; the rubber duck had just sunk the battleship when he noticed a white mark on his arm. He got a sponge and some soap and rubbed, but it didn't go. He rubbed some more, it was still there. "Aaaggghhh!" He let our an enormous scream. His wife came running, the servants came running. "What's the matter, what's the matter?" "I've got leprosy!" Now that was terrible. It meant he would have to leave his wife and family, his home, his job, all his men, the king and live all by himself. Wouldn't that be awful?

Spiritual concern and application

But you know we all suffer from a disease that's far worse than leprosy; it doesn't always keep us away from our family and friends, but it keeps us away from God and will eventually keep us out of heaven. It's called "I" disease* (explain), and it separates us from God.

As the general prepared to go, a little servant girl in his house told him about a man in her country who knew the living God, who she was sure would be able to heal the general. So he got permission from the king to go and try, and that was when he began to make . . . a general's MISTAKES. First he called his servants and made them pack suits of clothing and lots of money because he thought "If this man is going to heal me I will have to PAY". I meet a lot of people like that. They think they can pay God for their "I" disease by being good, but it doesn't work, does it, because we can never be good enough.

When the general and his men arrived in the far country, he thought, "I'm a very famous general, I should go to someone important", so he went to the king* and said, "I've come so you can heal me from my leprosy." "What, you've got leprosy? Guards quick, get him out of here!" The general was bounced out of the palace at once. You see he had gone to the wrong PERSON. We often try the wrong person to get rid of our "I" disease, but you know the vicar or priest or our teachers or parents can't get rid of it for us.

Then he went to the house of the man who knew God, but the prophet didn't come out to see him,

174

he just sent a messenger to say, "Go and wash in the river Jordan seven times."* The general was very angry, it was a horrible river, he didn't like the PLAN at all. God has a plan to get rid of our "I" disease but we don't like it because it means having to admit that we are wrong and saying sorry.

The general took off in his chariot and ended up down by the river where his soldiers persuaded him to try it. Yeuk! The river was revolting, all muddy and slimy, and he didn't like the PLACE. God's place for getting rid of "I" disease isn't very nice either. It looks like this.* When Jesus died on the cross he was being punished for all the things that anyone who believes and trusts in him has ever done wrong, all their "I" disease. The general went into the river and dipped seven times,* (act it out). "'Wow, fantastic I'm healed, it's gone, I'm clean!" He was so excited.

Response

I was just as excited when I said to Jesus "I'm sorry for all the wrong things I've done, please will you forgive me and make me clean inside?" Jesus did just that and I've been following him ever since. That's the most exciting thing you can ever do!

Creation

Today I would like to tell you the story of how the world began. In the beginning there was nothing except for God. Did you know that it was God who made everything? First of all God made the heavens and the earth. The earth was without any shape, it was all dark and there was water everywhere. God said 'Let there be light'', and straight away there was light (remove the black sheet over half of first picture). He separated the light and the dark. God called the light "day" and the dark "night". That was the end of the first day.

On the second day God put some of the water in the sky and left the rest on earth.*

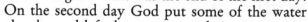

On the third day God put all the water on the earth in the same place so that land could appear. What is the name for the water that surrounds the land? Then God said that the land should be covered with grass, trees and flowers I'll draw them for you.* At the end of that day God looked at all the things he had made and was very pleased with them.

The fourth day God decided to decorate the world. Do you know what he put in the sky during the day to make things light?* And what did he put in the sky at night?*

The day after, he filled the sea; what with?* And
do you know what he put in the sky that fly?*
(You may have to explain that we made planes,
and at the moment we are talking about natural
things that God made in the beginning.)

On the sixth day God made all the animals.*
Then God decided to make something very special.
He decided to make man to be his friend.* Like
God we can think and decide things. Just as God
thought people were special when he made them,
today God thinks that you are very special and he
wants to be your friend.

God made a beautiful garden called Eden which
was full of trees, flowers and animals, with a little
river running through the middle of it. God put
Adam and Eve, the first people, in the garden with
everything they would need. Today God gives us
everything we need if we ask him. In the middle
of the garden there was a special tree, the tree of
knowledge of good and evil. God said they must
never eat its fruit or they would die. He said this
because he wanted Adam, Eve and each one of us
to listen to him and ask him what is good and bad.

In the garden there was also a serpent.* The
serpent was God's enemy, and wanted to destroy
the friendship between God and Adam and Eve.
He said to Eve,* "Did God really say you couldn't
eat the fruit from any tree in the garden?" Eve
said, "We can eat any fruit in the garden, except
from that one tree in the middle of the garden'.
"God just wants to spoil your fun", said the serpent. "Why not try the fruit from the tree of knowledge? It won't hurt." The fruit looked very tasty,
so Eve tried some and then gave some to Adam.

Later they realised what they had done: they had disobeyed God. We are all like them, we disobey our parents and God. God says that disobedience is bad, and it is because of all the bad things we do that we are separated from God. Because of their disobedience, Adam and Eve were frightened of God and hid in the garden. You know, when you have done something bad, you deserve to be punished, and often you are afraid of being punished.

When God came into the garden he found them straight away and he knew that they had eaten the fruit. Did you know that God knows all about you, that he knows all the good and bad things that you have done and that even so he loves you very much? God was sad that Adam and Eve had been disobedient, and because of their disobedience they had to leave the garden. God is sad when we choose to do naughty things, because they separate us from him and heaven. God loves you and he wants to give you the chance to be his friend. So God sent his son Jesus to take the punishment that we all deserve.* Jesus died on a cross and three days later he came back to life to show us that he was the Son of God. If you are prepared to say sorry to God for all the wrong things you have done, and to live as he wants you to, you can become his friend today. I asked Jesus to be my friend when I was only a little older than some of you. Those of you who want God to forgive you because of what Jesus has done can come to see me after the meeting.

32: A typical conjuring routine

The script was prepared by Peter Hodge, although something similar is used by most OAC evangelists. The trick described is one of the most effective for use in the open air. The technical details of conjuring are beyond the scope of this book: this script is included mainly to illustrate how to relate the trick and the "patter". Those wishing to learn to use the trick should consider buying it from a magician's supplier or attending a seminar on Christian conjuring.

The three block trick

Truth: A broken and restored relationship between us and God.

Props required

1. Three blocks, approximately 100–120mm (4–5″) across with a 15mm (5/8″) hole drilled through each block. These need to be painted, one gold, one green and one black (or scarlet).

2. Two pieces of soft magician's rope about 2 metres long.
3. A piece of red cloth about 700mm (24'') square.

Presentation

Ladies and gentlemen, today at no cost to the tax-payers, being performed without the means of a safety net; an unbelievable trick. The trick has to be seen to be believed. Required are just three wooden blocks and a couple of pieces of rope. I wonder sir would you mind examining this block (throwing the block to him gently). You will notice a few things sir. Firstly it's coloured gold, secondly it has a hole drilled through the middle and if you were to turn it over you would find there is a hole drilled through from that side also! (Do the same with the other two blocks, making similar light-hearted comments).

You might wonder why there is no charge for this stupendous trick. Well one, because I have enough of my own money to worry about let alone yours as well, also because I am a committed Christian and I want to use this trick to illustrate some truths. (As you sell yourself and the trick you start to move into the Truth aspects in the trick. Taking the two pieces of rope from around your neck, show them, stating that these remind you a little bit of life, they have a beginning and an end, so have our lives. They twist here and there, so do our lives.) I can remember a traumatic experience when I was 18 years old being told my dad had been knocked down by a car and killed whilst going to work that morning. Our lives twist here and they twist there, some things are good some not so good. These ropes are clean, God our creator desires our lives to be good and clean.

Sir, (looking at the person with the black/scarlet block) have you checked out the block? There is nothing peculiar? Great. Could you help me thread these two ropes through the hole in the block, and then hold the ends of them, thank you. (You now have an "assistant" out with you. Now get someone else in the crowd to hold the other ends. Hold up the black/scarlet block now in the middle of the rope. Explain that this block stands for the wrong in our lives. We don't shout about it but it stands out like a sore thumb! Now get the two ends of the rope (their choice of ends), and tie the black/scarlet block on with a single knot.)

Get the people with the other blocks to bring them out again getting them to put the blocks on the ropes. The green standing for life and living things and therefore man. Gold stands for God. He exists, whether you believe it or not doesn't change his existence!

Now what have we got here? Man (green block) separated by sin (black/scarlet block) from a holy God (gold block). Sin being tied into his life. A problem that can be solved. There is only one way back to God, that's by removing what is separating us from God. God's done something about that in sending his Son, (show red silk, explaining about the blood being shed and the life being given) who died on the cross so that we could be brought back to God, if we put our trust in him. (As you are saying this cover the three blocks with the cloth and get the two assistants to pull on their ropes.

181

The black block falls off, the green and the gold blocks are free together on the ropes). As you can see the relationship is restored between God and man because of what Jesus has done.

33: A typical ventriloquism routine

This script was prepared by Dawn Clancy

Props required

A Pelham puppet and a giant comb. Puppet begins in a suitcase.

Evangelist (E): I've got a friend who lives in a suitcase, and who really wants to see you all today. In fact, when I put him to bed last night, I told him we were coming here today and do you know, ten minutes later he was back downstairs all ready to go. I said, "You can't go yet, you've got to go to bed". He said he'd already been to bed, but I sent him back again. So, he's really excited about seeing you . . . would you like to see him?

(Open suitcase . . . snoring noise).

E: Oh dear, he's so excited about seeing you he's gone to sleep. Shall I just leave him asleep? No? OK, if I count to three, can you all shout "Horace" and wake him up? One . . . two . . . three . . .

(Open suitcase. . .snoring noise).

E: You'll have to try again, and this time I'll leave the lid of the suitcase open: One . . . two . . . three . . .

Horace (H): What's all that noise?
E: Well there's lots of boys and girls out here who want to see you.
H: (looking round) Where are we?
E: We're in Newtown.
H: Do you mean Newtown zoo?
E: No, what makes you say that?
H: Well look at all the monkeys!
E: Horace those aren't monkeys, they're boys and girls.
H: Oh yes, so they are.
E: Do you notice anything special about them, Horace?
H: No.
E: Look closely and you'll see that they all look very smart, as if they've all had their hair combed. When was the last time you combed your hair Horace?
H: Err. . .about six months ago I think.
E: I thought that was the case.
H: No, that's the case! (pointing to suitcase).
E: Well anyway, have you got a comb in your suitcase?
H: I think so.
E: What do you mean you think so?
H: I told you I haven't used it for six months.
E: Well could you have a look please and see if you can find one.

A typical ventriloquism routine

(Horace rummages and produces giant-sized comb).

H: Here it is.

E: Good, now comb your hair ... (Horace combs one side) ... now the other side ... (Horace combs other side and proceeds to comb Evangelist's hair) ... No! not my hair too!

H: But it needs combing.

E: Oh no it doesn't, now stop it at once.

H: Oh alright then.

E: Now Horace you've made yourself all nice and tidy outside, but what about your inside.

H: My inside, what's wrong with my inside?

E: Well, do you remember the last time you told me a lie?

H: Oh dear.

E: And do you remember the last time you took something that didn't belong to you?

H: Oh dear.

E: And do you remember the last time you got into a fight?

H: Oh dear, oh dear, oh dear ... all those things make me feel really bad inside, a real mess.

E: That's right, they do. How do you think you could clean up the mess?

H: I could drink some washing-up liquid.

E: Yeuk. That wouldn't clean up all the bad things you do, would it. What would it do? ... That's right, it would make you sick, Horace.

H: Yeuk!

E: Yes it would be yeuk, so what else do you think you could do?

H: Errr. . .I don't know.

E: Well I'll tell you what, we're going to have a

185

story now, and if you listen very carefully I think you'll find out what to do.

H: Really, will I? Are they all going to listen too?

E: Yes, they're all going to listen too, so say goodbye nicely to all the boys and girls.

H: Goodbye nicely.

E: No! That's not what I had in mind.

H: There isn't much in your mind anyway!

E: Say goodbye.

H: Not nicely?

E: No! not nicely.

H: O.K . . . Goodbye you rotten horrible lot.

E: Horace that's not what I meant either.

H: Well you should say what you mean shouldn't you. She's getting cross now. She's not very nice when she's cross.

E: No, and I shan't be very nice to you in a minute, now say goodbye.

H: Oh alright, Goodbye everybody, see you next time . . . AAAGGGHHH! (Horace is replaced in the suitcase, trapping his legs, he screams and then his legs are put in).

E: Now, Horace wants to hear the story, so let's see if we can help him to find out want to do about his problem. . .

34: Components for children's programmes

These ideas have been collated from many different sources. Further inspiration for sketch times can be found in children's comics. The list of memory verses is by no means exhaustive. Do not be afraid of abbreviating the verses, if this can be done without changing the meaning. The pictures for memory verses and quizzes can be elaborated according to your artistic prowess!

Sketch time

A Mexican on a bicycle

A giraffe walking
past a window

A well-used comb

A little boy with a big drum

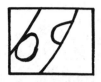

Mountain-ears

A Mexican frying an egg

A bear climbing a tree

An elephant sunbathing

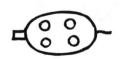

A false-alarm fire pole

A black eye

Memory verses

Num 32:23.
Josh 24:15.
Pss 23:1, 27:1, 28:7, 34:8; 37:4; 46:1; 46:10; 51:10; 55:22; 91:1; 103:1; 103:12; 105:4; 107:1; 118:8; 118:24; 119:105; 121:2; 126:3; 145:3; 150:6.
Prov 1:7; 3:5; 18:24; 28:20; 30:5.
Isa 43:11; 52:10; 55:6; 59:2.
Jer 32:27; 33:3.
Matt 11:28; 12:30.
Mark 1:15.
Luke 5:32; 11:28; 19:10.
John 1:29; 3:7; 3:16; 3:36; 6:37; 6:47; 7:37; 8:12; 8:32; 8:36; 10:9; 11:25; 14:6; 14:21.
Acts 16:31.
Rom 3:23; 5:8; 6:23; 8:28; 10:13.
1 Cor 15:3.
2 Cor 5:17; 6:2.
Gal 2:20; 3:11.
Eph 2:8.
Phil 1:21; 4:13.
1 Tim 1:15.
Titus 3:5.
Heb 11:6.
1 Peter 5:7.
1 John 5:12.
Rev 3:20.

Memory verse pictures

Mr Nosey: He climbs a ladder to see what is over the wall. Fill in the space under each rung as children get a letter wrong.

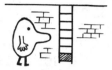

Winnie the Pooh: He eats a jar of honey each time they guess wrongly. Cross out one jar at a time.

Claude the crocodile: He eats the fish. Draw fish in his stomach or between his jaws.

Apple pie: A slice is eaten (coloured in) each time a mistake is made.

Sinking ship: she fills with water. Colour one section at a time.

Eclipse of the sun: it is covered by the shadow of the moon. Paint in successive segments.

Balloons: they burst. Cross out one at a time, and encourage the children to provide appropriate sound effects.

Glass of water: it is filled to overflowing. Paint in the water from the bottom upwards.

Components for children's programmes

Quiz Pictures

Snakes and ladders: throw a dice and advance a counter with each correct answer.

Noughts and crosses: This game is rather short so you may wish to play twice.

Blockbusters: each hexagon has a corresponding question, the answer beginning with the letter in the hexagon. Teams take it in turns to choose a hexagon, which will be coloured if a correct answer is given. One team attempts to make a horizontal line, the other a vertical line.

Clowns: a feature is added to the team's clown with each correct answer.

35: An outline of a typical 5-day club

This outline has been provided by Mike Gatley

Exploration Mount Sinai: Coming face to face with God

Day 1. "Setting off"
Spiritual content (SC): Release from slavery, turning your back on a sinful life. (2 Cor 5:17, Isa 59:2).
Memory verse (MV): Romans 6:23 "For the wages of sin is death but the gift of God is eternal life."

Day 2. "Danger along the way – the Red Sea. God goes before us"
SC: An impossible situation, we can't save ourselves.
MV: Proverbs 3:6 "In all your ways acknowledge him and he will make your paths straight."

Day 3. "Instruction – the Ten Commandments".
SC: Personal instructions, obedience (John 10:27).
MV: John 15:14 "You are my friends if you do what I command."

Day 4. "Facing the enemy – spies into Canaan".

SC: Having Jesus with us all the time
MV: Hebrews 13:5 "God has said never will I leave you."

Day 5. "Continuing the journey into the promised land".
SC: Heaven, eternal life
MV: John 1:12 "To all who received him he gave the right to become children of God."

Teams

Red – Joshua Giants.
Yellow – Caleb Conquerors.
Blue – Moses Marauders.
Green – Aaron Attackers.

Score Chart: Desert scene with four people to walk across it.

Publicity: Explorers need to sign up for an incredible journey across the wilderness. Must be ready to face danger and excitement. Sign on at (time) until (time) from Monday (date) to Friday (date). All explorers must be aged 5 to 11. Exploration headquarters, (church).

Badges: Triangular card shapes for the children to decorate as mountains.

36: Bibliography and further reading

Evangelism in general

Evangelism-now and then, Michael Green, IVP, 1979.

I believe in evangelism, David Watson, Hodder and Stoughton, 1979

Evangelism explosion, D. James Kennedy, EE, 1970.

Evangelism and the sovereignty of God, J. I. Packer, IVP, 1961

How to give away your faith, Paul E. Little, IVP, 1971.

Out of the saltshaker, Rebecca Manley-Pippert, IVP, 1979.

Apologetics

Evidence that demands a verdict, Josh McDowell, Agape Europe, 1972.

Issues facing Christians today, John Stott, Marshall, Morgan and Stott, 1984.

Bibliography and further reading

The history of open-air evangelism

The journal of John Wesley, abridged by Christopher Idle, Lion, 1986.

George Whitefield and the Great Awakening, John Pollock, Lion, 1972.

Great Revivals: God's men and their message, Colin Whittaker, Marshalls, 1984.

Open-air evangelism today

Preaching and painting the Gospel, Graham Simms.

Preaching and painting the Gospel 2, Graham Simms.

Sermons in paint for children, Graham Simms.

The fisherman's basket, Noel C. Gibson.

(All available from OAC GB)

Presenting Jesus in the open air, Mike Sprenger, Word Publishing 1983

A handbook on open-air evangelism, Edwin Baker, from The Open-Air Mission, 19 John St., London WC1N 2DZ.

A guide to child evangelism, Alan Bailey, from OAC Ministries, Box 1073, Banks Town, NSW, 2200 Australia.

Sketch and Tell, Keith Thompson, from ANZEA, 3 Richmond Rd., Homebush West, NSW, Australia.

Music

Make Way handbook for organisers and musicians, Graham Kendrick, Make Way Music.

Drama

Time to act, Paul Burbridge and Murray Watts, Hodder Christian Paperbacks, 1979.
Lightning sketches, Paul Burbridge and Murray Watts, Hodder Christian Paperbacks 1981.

Conjuring and escapology

Magigram magazine, the Supreme Magic Co. Ltd, Supreme House, Bideford, Devon EX39 2AN. Telephone 0237–479266.
(The Supreme Magic Company is a secular organisation from whom many evangelists purchase their conjuring materials. Magigram includes a Gospel magic column. Supreme also publish a number of booklets on various forms of conjuring and escapology.)
Christian Conjurer magazine, The Fellowship of Christian Magicians, Mail Center, PO Box 1027, Wheaton, Illinois 60189.1027, USA.
(Further information about the Fellowship of Christian Magicians can be obtained from Henry Smith, 14 Barle Close, Taunton, Somerset TA1 2NY.)

Ventriloquism

Gottle o' geer!, Ray Alan, Pagoda 1987

Counselling literature

Return to God (for adults), Peter Hodge.
Return to God (for children), Peter Hodge.

Bibliography and further reading

Going God's Way, Peter Hodge.
(Available from OAC Wales, 51 Moy Road, Roath,
Cardiff CF2 4SH, Wales.)